BUILD
EXCITE
IGNITE

TESTIMONIALS

After 25 years in this industry of creating our own income and empowering others to work for themselves, I've crossed paths with many self-appointing gurus and so-called experts that are teaching from theory and textbooks and regurgitating what they are hearing from others.

Jim is not that guy. Jim has been there and done that. Jim operates with integrity, character, and even a big splash of fun. So for real results, practical application, and a realistic view of what it takes to create your own profits and not hate every work day, read this book and apply its principles to your own efforts.

– **Carrie Wilkerson, Author, International Speaker, and Business Consultant**

Jim, I want to express my heartfelt appreciation for sharing your knowledge and insights through your book. Your passion for expansion, growth, and empowering others truly shines through your work. It has been an absolute pleasure witnessing your work, and I genuinely admire your unwavering dedication to guiding individuals to personal fulfilment and success.

– **Jo Wise, MCC, ICF Trainer, and Executive Leadership Coach**

Dedicated, committed, enthusiastic, Jim brings the knowledge and capabilities that only experience can build. Jim is renowned for making the complex simple because he moves step by step as a guide through the maze of essentials to build a successful, efficient, and profitable business. When you have a business to grow, you want Jim on your team!

– Joanne Clark, Director and Master Trainer NLP, Destiny Pursuit

The industry needs more great people changing lives. But the biggest gap is going from healer, helper, or coach to business owner. Jim closes this gap; that's why we recommend him to all of our students.

– Justin O'Hehir, Director of Inspired Results and Chair of the NLPAA

Having Jim as a member of our training faculty has supported hundreds of our students to overcome the challenges they have faced in shaping their businesses.
It has been great to see students use his simple systems and support to grow faster in the industry and become confident entrepreneurs.

– Glen Murdoch, Founder of The Life Coaching College

I've had the honour of knowing Jim for 15 years and have watched him create a powerful business with epic client results. His vision for our industry and his dogged determination to ensure his clients' success is a gift to everyone he works with and our entire industry. He is a true leader! (He's also just an all-around stand-up guy!).

– Brody Lee, CEO of Beyond Impact

You know that feeling when you're trapped in a job that sucks the life out of you? Jim Cocks does. He's been there, done that, and bought the T-shirt. But here's the kicker: he turned it all around.

After experiencing serious burnout, Jim didn't just bounce back; he soared. And now he's helping others do the same with his coaching business.

See, Jim isn't just a coach; he's a game changer, a guiding light in the foggy world of transitioning from being a coach to a successful entrepreneur. You think you're just a coach? Nah, you're a business owner, and Jim's here to show you how to do it right.

His book, Build Excite Ignite, *is like your GPS to success. He's taken his journey from zero to a million-dollar coaching enterprise and laid it out for all of us to learn from. And trust me, this isn't your typical rah-rah self-help book. It's real; it's raw, and it's packed with practical advice you can put into action today.*

So, whether you're feeling stuck or just need a little push to take your coaching business to the next level, grab a cup of coffee, get comfy, and dive into this book. And remember, success isn't a solo gig. With Jim by your side, you'll be ready to face the tough questions, create action, and get your coaching business where you want it to be.

– Toni Bache, Business Strategist for seven-figure companies

Listening and caring are the hallmarks of a good teacher, coach, or mentor. Jim takes these skills to the next level by breaking down complex concepts and making them into small, actionable steps that his students can then put into place. Jim empowers his students, which, in turn, allows them to grow and flourish with confidence.

– Heather Roberts, Founder of Extraordinary Women

JIM COCKS

BUILD
EXCITE
IGNITE

How to Beat Burnout and Build a Six-Figure Business in 12 Months

First published in 2023 by Dean Publishing
PO Box 119
Mt. Macedon, Victoria, 3441
Australia
deanpublishing.com

Copyright © Jim Cocks

All rights reserved. No part of this publication may be reproduced, stored in a retrieval system or transmitted in any way or by any means, electronic, mechanical, photocopying, recording or otherwise, without the prior written permission of the publisher.

Cataloguing-in-Publication Data
National Library of Australia
Title: Build Excite Ignite: How to Beat Burnout and Build a Six-Figure Business in 12 Months
Edition: 1st edn
ISBN: 978-1-92545-266-2
Category: Business/entrepreneurship/personal development

The views and opinions expressed in this book are those of the author and do not necessarily reflect the official policy or position of any other agency, publisher, organization, employer or company. Assumptions made in the analysis are not reflective of the position of any entity other than the author(s) — and, these views are always subject to change, revision, and rethinking at any time.

The author, publisher or organizations are not to be held responsible for misuse, reuse, recycled and cited and/or uncited copies of content within this book by others.

Dedication

To my dad, for teaching me that
no matter what life throws at you,
you can always find a way to overcome it.

CONTENTS

Let's Keep This Intro Brief.. 1

PART 1: FAILING FORWARD – THE LITERAL STORY OF MY LIFE
Chapter 1: Corporate Dream Turned Nightmare............. 11
Chapter 2: Coaching? What's That? 23

PART 2: MINDSET
Chapter 3: The Biggest Barrier to Success 45
Chapter 4: Money Mindset.. 57
Chapter 5: Blueprint for an Unstoppable Mindset
(Tips, Tricks and Strategies)... 63

PART 3: BUILD
Chapter 6: Nail Your Niche.. 83
Chapter 7: Craft Your Offer.. 103

PART 4: EXCITE
Chapter 8: Lead Magnets Attract 127
Chapter 9: Getting Your Message Across........................ 135
Chapter 10: Crafting Compelling Content...................... 157

PART 5: IGNITE
Chapter 11: Sharpen Your Sales Mindset........................ 175
Chapter 12: The Ultimate Lead Journey.......................... 187

Epilogue: The Final Act.. 205
About the Author.. 208
Jim's Clients 209

LET'S KEEP THIS INTRO BRIEF...

THE LEVEL UP CREED

It starts with **BELIEF**. Belief in yourself. To continuously learn new **SKILLS** and **IMPROVE** your craft. To **CHALLENGE** yourself daily to continually **LEARN, GROW, INNOVATE**, and **IMPROVE**. Follow your **PASSIONS** and outgrow your comfort zone. Be **DRIVEN** internally and externally. **DREAM** so big it scares you. **TRUST** the process, have **FUN**, and be **COACHABLE**. Be **ACCOUNTABLE** for every action you take or don't take. Knowing that what you **DO** says who you **ARE**. You don't complain but strive to be **SOLUTION ORIENTED**. Be **INDEPENDENT**, ask questions, and seek support when stuck. Be responsible for your own **RESULTS** rather than blaming others. Be **GENEROUS**, share what is working, and encourage others. **YOU LOVE BUILDING YOUR BUSINESS**. You work to create a **POSITIVE IMPACT** in the world. You accept its about **PROGRESS NOT PERFECTION**. You understand that **SUCCESSFUL PEOPLE** don't do it alone. You take on every **CHALLENGE** and embrace the fear. Because through overcoming your challenges you create **SUCCESS**. You practise what you **PREACH**. Seeing people not only for who they are but for whom they can **BECOME**. Striving to live with **INTEGRITY, SELF-DISCIPLINE**, and **PASSION** in every area of your life. Make **SUCCESS** your only option. You commit to **LEVEL UP**.

I'm not a big fan of fluff. I'm a straight to the point kind of guy. I don't see writing a book as an opportunity to waffle on and fill your head with even more information that isn't going to (a) give value to you and (b) help you take some serious action (the more important of the two). That's the point of this book: to give value that drives you to take action so you can generate the momentum you need to quit the corporate rat-race – that is, if you're ready to be your own boss – and build and Level Up your business faster. If you're ready to make more of an impact in the world and create the freedom you want, then you've already taken the first major step by picking up this book.

I'll share some of my knowledge – but I won't stop there. I'll also provide you with the tools you need to scale a million-dollar business, whether you're at the startup stage or have an established business that's ready for serious growth. Even seven-figure entrepreneurs need to work on their offer, along with many other things. If you're willing to do the work, then you *will* make it happen, provided you've got grit and determination in high supply. It's as simple as that. The energy you put out into the world will eventually come back.

So, what is the Level Up Formula? I'm glad you asked! The Level Up Formula is a system I originally developed to help coaches take their businesses to the next level. What does that look like? More freedom. Bigger impact. And of course, serious profit. We're building your dream life here. *That's* the goal. That's what it's all about. So, are you with me?

Although we mainly work with coaches, or people who want to add coaching products to their offering, in all honesty, you can apply our tools and training to almost any service-based business. We've worked with consultants, therapists, trainers, healers, even animal communicators who went from selling $60, one-hour sessions to $5,000 packages. For real. You don't need to be a coach to benefit from Level Up. You could be a hairdresser, a masseuse, a plastic surgeon – it doesn't matter. If you want to avoid burnout, be your own boss, serve people, and leverage your time, you can Level Up your business using the tools and advice in this book. But hey, I was a mindset coach before I began coaching coaches and helping people escape corporate, so the coaching industry is where my heart lies. Cool? Great!

That's enough about me. Don't worry, you'll get to know me intimately in **Part 1** of this book, where I talk to you with full, unfiltered vulnerability about my climb up the corporate ladder, my drug addiction, and my catastrophic rock-bottom moment. I promise it's not as bleak as it sounds. *Spoiler alert* – there *is* a happy ending. But you already knew that, right? If I hadn't managed to get my shit together, this book wouldn't exist. But it does. I'm here. And if there's one thing I've learnt in my entrepreneurial journey, it's that successful people don't do it alone. So, if you're happy to let me provide you with a few shortcuts to success, I'm happy to provide them. Shall we say, I'm an open book?

Now, let's talk about *you*. You have an entrepreneurial spark, but perhaps you've not yet utilised it to its full potential. You may be feeling stuck in a 9 to 5 (or maybe it's more like an 8 to 8, and you have no life), working yourself to the bone for someone else's gain, with no finish line in sight. Perhaps you've already dropped out of the rat-race, started your own business, and you're ready to scale and create a massive impact in the world. Whatever stage of your journey you're at, I've got you covered.

Now, I know not all businesses and industries are the same, so, as we go, I want you to use a little creativity and imagine how the advice in this book applies to your unique situation. Don't feel boxed in by the words *I've* chosen to use. Treat it like a choose your own adventure. You're in control. Don't forget it.

So, we've already established that you have an entrepreneurial spark, and you're ready to – figuratively – ignite the world with your awesome enterprise. You're determined to succeed in your industry – perhaps you're already succeeding – but you haven't quite got a grip on all aspects of scaling a business. To be fair, it ain't as easy as it used to be. These days, we've got so many things to consider. Business systems. Marketing strategies. Multiple avenues of communication. Not to mention, all the tech stuff. We've got social media. Content creation. Online coaching platforms. AI that can do a lot of the work for us. How do we even begin to wrap our heads around all that? Cue overwhelm, cue frustration, cue too hard basket... *swish*.

Sound full-on? Absolutely! Is it really? Not exactly. I guarantee that by the end of this book, you'll have your head so thoroughly wrapped around the most important aspects of running and scaling a business that you'll barely recognise yourself.

It all starts with **Mindset**. It's the key to everything, which is why you'll find a big, meaty mindset section towards the beginning of the book, right after my bleak story with the happy ending. If you can master your mindset, you've already overcome the most difficult part of growing a successful business, the part that causes most people to fail.

Do you want to help more people and make a bigger

impact in the world? Do you want to consistently bring in five to six figures per month? All of this is totally possible. Hey, I did it, and I use the same exact formula to support our Level Up members to do it all the time. We're moving from possible to probable territory here. But to **Build** a business that's set up to scale, you first need to lay a solid foundation. We're talking about nailing your niche, crafting your offer, and everything else required to put you on the path to success.

We're going to break down everything you need to know to **Excite** your audience and craft a brand that truly resonates. Attracting your ideal client is about more than what your business does. It's also about who you are. Why do you think I dedicated a good chunk of this book to telling my story? I wanted to put it all on the table: my successes, my failures, and my most crushing moments – my most *human* moments. We're all human, yeah? Assuming aliens aren't already among us. Your story *is* important, and vulnerability is the key to unlocking connection with your ideal clients.

Do you want to have absolute confidence in your sales process? Do you want to craft an offer so good it sells itself? We're going to **Ignite** your sales by applying the same tools and techniques we use at Level Up to get our clients.

I'm not holding anything back with this book. I wrote this as a standalone resource you can use to Level Up every aspect of your business. But you're not just levelling up your business. You're levelling up yourself. Your mindset. Your sales and marketing strategies. While I couldn't realistically pack every piece of the Level Up Formula into this book, I've included enough value to create a serious impact in your business and your life.

All right, you've been warned. This book requires action so if you're not willing to do the work, you can put this book down right now...

Are you still with me? Great!

Do the activities. The worksheets, they're there for a reason. I don't want to sound like your high school teacher here but... "Do your homework!" You'll get the best results not just by reading, but by doing, too. You've got to take action. It's the only way to truly move forward.

Jim is sharing more in his BONUS MATERIAL.

See exclusive downloads, videos, audios and photos.

DOWNLOAD it now at
clearedgecoaching.com.au/beitraining

PART 1

FAILING FORWARD – THE LITERAL STORY OF MY LIFE

It's story time! Are you excited? I am. Vulnerability was a big thing for me when I was stepping into the world of coaching. I was a big believer in the idea that I had to do the work if I wanted to create transformations in others, and, to be totally honest, I was tired of living a lie. It was time to drop the pride, the outer persona, and show the real, authentic me. And, man, was that a HUGE weight lifted from my shoulders. Not only that, but I started to find 'my people' and felt like after years of not quite fitting in, I was finally a part of a tribe. Funny that – when you show your true, authentic self, you meet true, authentic people. I've been through some shit – who hasn't? But I've come out the other side, hopefully not smelling too bad.

So, let's get into it.

Chapter 1

CORPORATE DREAM TURNED NIGHTMARE

Big corporate income = freedom

Debunked!

I started my career as a performer, working as a singer and dancer in musical theatre. In a way, I still am a performer, especially when I'm up on stage, training hundreds of coaches. There's just a lot less singing and dancing now. Most of the time, anyway. As a performer, I loved the freedom and flexibility the job provided. A six-month contract could take me to Singapore, Tokyo Disneyland, or have me travelling all over, visiting amazing cities and meeting amazing people. What a life! Ah, but there's always a catch, isn't there? If something sounds too good to be true – well, you know the rest.

For me, the problem was that I never had consistent income. One minute, I'd be performing in front of a big, awesome crowd in Japan; the next, I'd be back home, making coffee at a local cafe or working reception at my local gym. Yes, coffee is awesome too – no one knows that as well as me – but steaming milk and grinding beans doesn't quite provide the same thrill as bouncing around on stage, singing my heart out to a captivated audience. The contrast was severe, and the endless uncertainty prompted me to make a drastic career change. Saying farewell to the stage for now, I moved to Sydney to study my MBA and step into the corporate world.

AN EMPTY JOURNEY UP THE CORPORATE LADDER

While performing, I also began my training career as a dance teacher. Even then, I loved supporting people to learn, to grow, and to take the necessary steps to discover exactly what they wanted to do and to find and actually live their passion. So, when the time came, I fell into leadership easily. My first role as an assistant manager was at a factory outlet clothing store. Denim everywhere! After that, I moved from company to company, levelled up to manager, regional, then state. It was great for a while, but I always got bored. Whenever I'd spent a certain amount of time in a job, usually a year or so, I found myself asking:

"What now?"

"Where can I find the next shiny, new role?"

"Who's going to feed my appetite for growth and development next?"

Sound familiar?

Some might just blame my ADHD, but, for me, knowledge was like fast food. Eat some, digest, and I'd be hungry again an hour later. That's why I switched jobs so

1

CORPORATE DREAM TURNED NIGHTMARE

often. I needed that next serving of knowledge, that next boost to my mental blood sugar. Doing the same thing day in, day out just didn't satisfy my appetite. I always craved the next challenge, the next opportunity to learn and grow, and I would either get a promotion or jump to a completely different company. But the restlessness always returned. My MO (modus operandi) was to find a new manager or mentor, suck their brain juices dry of everything they knew, and then move on to the next person I could learn from. I was a brain-eating zombie! I know that sounds bad, but it's how it was. I was blindly running the rat-race and fulfilling my need for growth by constantly seeking that next shiny, new thing to learn. I never truly felt fulfilled until I became a full-time coach. To my unfortunate victims, I apologise. I truly appreciate everything I learnt from you. Whether you taught me what to do or what not to do, it got me here today.

As a performer, I got paid to travel, which was amazing. When I began my corporate career, I still wanted to see the world, so I chased a bigger income. For over a decade, this was my biggest motivator: striving to reach that next rung of the ladder and earn more money. Once I had a six-figure income, I would have the freedom to do what I wanted, right? *Wrong.* If there's one thing working a 9 to 5, Monday to Friday (or 8 to 7, Monday to Sunday) job doesn't provide, it's freedom. Yeah, it took me a while to figure that out. *Don't* fall into the same trap. If you just said to yourself, "I'm already there," GET OUT NOW!

At the time, the equation seemed simple: high income = freedom. Therefore, chasing a six-figure salary was a worthy pursuit, right? Not exactly. Certainly not in my case. The more I earned, the more my responsibilities, and the work week, grew. I was strapped to a chair, chained to

> **The zest is in the journey and not in the destination.**

RALPH DELAHAYE PAINE

1

CORPORATE DREAM TURNED NIGHTMARE

a desk, my eyes glued to a screen – a brutal image, I know – sometimes putting in a solid 80 hours per week. But at least I was earning my freedom, right? Nope. One of my bosses, who ended up being my last, told me I could never take more than ten days off at a time because they needed me too much. And there it was. My plan to clock up some annual leave and spend six weeks in Europe blew up in my face. I was shattered. Here I was, literally working myself to death, and my goal of travelling the world was further from reach than ever before. But hey, at least I had that nice, big salary, right? Yep, I was living the dream. Not my dream though. Someone else's, perhaps.

I didn't realise at the time that a lot of my behaviour was centred around people-pleasing. If you're familiar with DISC personality profiles, I'm a high I (influencer), which means I'm a people person. I want to make everyone happy, and, at this stage of the story, I wanted everyone to love me. I always felt that I had to give, give, give, even at the cost of my own needs, happiness, and wellbeing. I wasn't filling my own cup first. How can you serve others from an empty cup? You can't. It's that simple. It may sound selfish, but you really have to put yourself first if you truly want to help others. That's right. You heard it here. I'm totally giving you permission to be selfish. Or, as Oprah so rightly implies, it's okay to be full of yourself. When people say she's full of herself, she takes it as a compliment, and so do I. Isn't it refreshing? Don't feel bad about doing things for you. Don't feel guilty for taking a little me time. Don't hesitate to fill your own cup first so you can better serve others. Take it from someone who spent years walking around with an empty cup. You *must* put yourself first. No arguments. No exceptions. No compromises. I know the givers among us will object

– hello, old me – but self-care is paramount. Period. Had I realised this sooner, I might not have turned to drugs and partying to fill that void.

THE EASY ESCAPE

Have you ever been promised the world, only to end up with something that doesn't even come close? We've all been there.

You might see an advertisement that unashamedly oversells a fantastic new product. "Buy this thing! It's great! It will solve X problem like magic!" Who doesn't want a magic pill? I'm certainly not going to suggest doing something the hard way if *magic* is the solution. Who would? So, you pull out your credit card, punch in your details, and hit that BUY NOW button before you can consider whether the claims might just be a little overstated.

A few days later, you realise you still haven't opened and explored that shiny new thing yet. So, you 'unbox' your miracle product and take it for a spin. Hmm... something isn't right. Perhaps *you're* doing something wrong, so you read the instructions and try again. Nothing changes. Sure, it's doing *something*, but it's far from magical. At least, it's not Harry Potter level of magic. It's more "some kid bought a beginner's magic kit, practised for an afternoon, and decided to put on a show" kind of magic. And when he pulls the rabbit out of the hat, it's not looking so hot. It was white and fluffy in the picture, but this one looks like it has been rolling around in a dusty field, and it's missing its left ear. The promise doesn't match reality. Three weeks later, it's dead. I know I probably lost a few of you with the dead rabbit analogy – I apologise! I love animals! – but hang in there. It's integral to the story, as that was my corporate experience: a series of dead rabbits.

Whenever I took a new job or promotion, it never turned out to be quite what was advertised. In my last role in 'people and culture' – the more appropriate term for human resources – I was told I would be building onboarding systems and completely changing the company's cultural landscape. But the reality was so much different. While the old-school board members had *said* they wanted someone who could create change, it turned out that wasn't what they actually wanted. What they really wanted was to create the illusion of championing change without actually creating the change. Clever, right? That's corporate for you. Once I took the job, I found myself completely hamstrung, and I couldn't create the impact I desired. Another dead rabbit.

Our brains are hardwired to focus on the negative. It's a survival instinct. Although every promotion meant my salary and responsibilities increased, a year in, I struggled to focus on anything but the negative aspects, the terrible tricks performed by questionable corporate magicians. I was creating *some* change, but I rarely had time to enjoy my success. I was trying to convince myself that every step up the corporate ladder was a win. And it was, right? Even if it meant longer hours, more stress, and a deeper descent into a negative mental space. I needed an escape, but I couldn't get it the way I wanted, so, naturally, I turned to drugs, alcohol, and partying on weekends. If I couldn't fill my figurative cup, at least I could fill, and then empty, my literal cup. Fantastic solution. What could possibly go wrong?

On my mission to escape the stress of corporate life at any cost, I fell in with what some might label 'the wrong crowd'. The guy I was dating at the time even later became a drug dealer. For me and the people I was hanging out with, drugs were a big part of life. My mindset, my relationships, and my behaviour were all about blanking out and avoiding reality. I might not have admitted it to myself at the time, but I wasn't happy with what I was doing day-to-day or where my life was going. I would drink and take drugs on weekends to feel better about the work week but when Monday came around, I would feel like absolute crap – I was great at hiding it, by the way – which, as I'm sure you can imagine, didn't help my mental state at all. So, work stress was fuelling my partying, and partying was adding to my work stress. To you playing at home, the solution likely seems simple: stop taking drugs and change careers. Makes sense, right? But after trying that again and again, always ending up back where I started, I knew the solution wouldn't come easily, not without help.

Big income doesn't necessarily equal freedom. I had learnt that much at least. But because I couldn't solve the seemingly complex equation of how to be happy and gain the freedom I wanted, I fell into a simpler pattern. Friday nights, I would get home, go out, party, spend the next two days recovering from a hangover, struggle to get up for work on Monday, then push through another week so I could party again. Looking back, I don't know how I did it. The past often feels like that, yeah? We look back at a difficult time and wonder how the hell we managed to drag ourselves through it. But we did. Somehow. And we'd do it again if we had to. Don't doubt that for a second. Our past struggles make us who we are today: stronger, wiser, and better equipped to deal with the next set of life's challenges. Those challenges will *always* come. It's what makes life so satisfying. I'm serious. If it were too easy, we'd all get bored and wouldn't want to stick around for long. Or we would find a way to make life more challenging for us. I've found there's a sweet spot between too much and not enough challenge, and drifting too far in either direction can cause problems. Anyway, back to the story.

You can probably guess what happened next. It shouldn't come as a surprise. Well, it did to me, but I was a special case. I was too close to the action. "When did you hit rock bottom?", you might be asking. Great question! Surely, working yourself into a state of utter misery and taking drugs every weekend isn't sustainable in the long-term, right? Like I said, I went for the simple solution – it just happened to be wrong. After partying hard for roughly two years, I finally met the end result of my miscalculation and hit rock bottom at full force.

SELF-DESTRUCT COMPLETE

Clearly, I never fit into the corporate system, but it wasn't just the long hours, broken promises, and lack of freedom that didn't work for me. My ambition was also a problem. That's right. I was *too* ambitious, always trying to move the dial quicker than my bosses were willing to allow. If you've ever worked in corporate, you'll understand what I mean. Change is scary. It comes with risks. Few people fear those risks more than the executives at a big business that's already doing well. *Why fix what ain't broke?* That's the corporate mindset. It's limiting. It's uninspiring. It's downright unentrepreneurial. Where I saw huge potential, they saw disruption to the status quo. Why push the dial when everything's already super great? Why? Because it could be *better*. Much better. But change makes certain people uncomfortable, so I could never create the impact I wanted in the corporate system. That's why working for myself always appealed to me. If only I'd had the courage to take the plunge sooner. Hey, I got there in the end. I just took the scenic route. Something about the journey being more important than the destination... You know what I'm talking about.

At the time, I couldn't deal with the uncertainty of leaving my corporate career to start my own business. I didn't even know what my own business would look like, so, instead, I spent a good seven years standing on various rungs of the corporate ladder. But no matter how high I climbed, the view always sucked. In fact, it often got worse. I'm sure you can imagine the things I had to tell myself to keep climbing. *The view will be nicer higher up. I must be close to the good rung now. Better work harder!* The cognitive dissonance was real.

Towards the end of my corporate career, I would sit in my car and scream my lungs out before walking into the office, which probably should have been a warning sign that something was wrong. If not to me, to anyone walking past who happened to hear it. What a sight (and sound) I must have been! But sitting in my car and screaming simply became another part of my regular workday routine. Rock bottom incoming.

High stress. Drugs. Alcohol. Poor sleep. Terrible mental state. What's this a recipe for? If you answered, "Complete mental breakdown," you'd be absolutely right. Eventually, I reached a breaking point where I couldn't do it anymore. The stress and anxiety were too much to bear, and the drugs no longer helped (as if they ever did). Another promotion would only add weight to a back that was already breaking. All of my simple solutions had failed. What was left? Tough choices. Difficult decisions. Walking away from everything I had worked for. Drastic change, like the type I had pushed for in my corporate gigs, was the only option I had left. It was time to jump off the ladder. Not literally. Although, at my lowest point, I did consider it. Thankfully, I had two people who would support me no matter what.

I vividly remember walking out of the office one day and standing in a park, where I called my parents and explained the situation. I told them if something didn't change, I probably wouldn't be on this planet much longer. That authentic honesty opened my inner floodgates, and I think I cried for the first time in roughly nine years. I joke now about jumping off a ladder, but that really was how bad it got. After speaking with my parents, I handed in my resignation that day and walked away from the corporate world, just like that. Two weeks later, Mum and Dad drove all the way from Melbourne to Sydney, threw me in the back of a van – perhaps not so dramatically – and I began the long road to getting my life back on track.

The burnout and depression hit me hard. I spent six months in bed before I could even begin to plan my next move. Luckily, I had some money saved up for the holiday I was never allowed to take – a positive after all! – which meant I could survive without an income for a while. Not knowing what I would do next was terrifying. For almost six months, I was paralysed with uncertainty. I watched every possible series and movie I could on Netflix and when I wasn't doing that, I was playing video games. I was too mentally drained to think about the future. But thanks to my parents' support, simply holding space for me, a future *was* possible. I just had to figure out what it would look like.

Chapter 2
COACHING? WHAT'S THAT?

Coaches are just unschooled therapists

I wish I had discovered coaching sooner. If I had been able to reach out and talk to someone during my darkest days, I know it would have helped, and I wouldn't have self-destructed as much as I did. This is why I'm so passionate about what I do now. Instead of focusing on the 200 or so people a year that I could coach, why not support 200 coaches and other entrepreneurs who want to make a positive impact in the world? Through them, the impact we could create together would be, well, 200 times what I could do on my own. I've witnessed the amazing transformations coaches can provide, but the ones who succeed are those who do the work themselves. Coaching wasn't on my radar until a friend in Sydney recommended that *I* see a coach. I was more than a little sceptical at first.

"A coach? What, is that like a therapist?" I had been badly burned by psychologists in the past, so I was hesitant to risk that route again. But the more I learnt, the clearer the differences became.

Therapists often tell us what to do based on their own knowledge and experience, and I had a few who led me down the wrong track. I'm not saying therapists don't have a purpose and a place, but they never worked for me. Coaching, however, is so much more empowering. It's about owning your shit and being empowered to make the changes you know you need to make. A coach believes their client is not broken; they have the answers and are doing the best with the tools they have right now. Our job is to help them embrace the fear and create the changes and shifts they need to succeed. My story is a perfect example. I knew I had to stop taking drugs, and I knew I had to find another job, but the habits and patterns I had created in my life were easier to succumb to than creating positive change. I wasn't ready to face the truth, but a good coach could have helped me excavate through my bullshit and bring to light critical answers I hadn't quite managed to unearth on my own. I could have stepped onto a better path sooner. How many people could have saved themselves a lot of time and trouble if they had known about coaching? If they had seen a coach? If they had discovered their truths sooner? *A lot*. No doubt in my mind. Does everyone *need* a coach? Not necessarily. But successful people don't do it alone. Why do life the hard way when we don't have to? We are creatures built on connection and contribution. Success comes so much easier when we have a little help along the way. We don't have to go it alone. While I don't consider myself a slow learner, it took me a while to realise that. Letting go of the ego and the fear of being judged was the first step.

Therapists, mentors, and coaches – what's the difference? I mean, what's it really like to seek help from the people in these professions? What does the experience look like? I like to use an analogy about buying a bicycle in my trainings. It goes something like – actually, let's scrap the bike analogy and try something a little different. Here we go. So, a *therapist*, a *mentor*, and a *coach* walk into a bar. Stay with me now. A patron is standing at the bar, looking rather confused.

"Is something wrong?" the therapist asks.

"I don't know what drink to buy," the guy says.

"Well," says the therapist, "let's talk about your past. What drinks have you consumed previously?"

The patron lists all the drinks he has drunk in the past, and the therapist supports him to uncover why he enjoyed experiencing those drinks. But he still doesn't know what action to take, what drink to buy.

Please note, before I go on with my tale, there is a place for all types of support, be it therapists, consultants, teachers, and so on. They can each complement the practices of a coach, depending on the stage of life someone is at. Coaching is *not* therapy. I want to make that clear. All right, let's continue.

Next, the mentor comes over and says, "Let me help you out. These are the drinks I've had in the past..." And he proceeds to list all of his favourite drinks. "I always order a martini. Vodka, not gin. I like it, so you will too."

The patron orders a martini, takes a sip, and frowns. "This doesn't taste how he said it would."

"Of course it doesn't," the coach says, having overheard the conversation. "Everyone's tastes are different, so you can't just go by what someone else likes. Tell me, why do you want a drink? What are you here to celebrate? Have you tried any drinks recently? Which ones did you like? *Why* did you like them? Do you have friends here? What are they drinking? Would you like to give one of those drinks a try?"

The questions surprise the patron – seriously, who puts that much thought into ordering a drink? – but he answers them as best as he can.

"All right, great," the coach says. "Let's sample a few different drinks, and you'll know which one is right for you." The coach sits with the patron as he selects a few different drinks from the menu. After about 30 minutes, the patron has found his beverage of choice: a non-alcoholic gin and tonic.

"Great, you did it!" the coach says.

"You could have just asked me," the bartender says, an older, smartly dressed woman, with slicked back hair, who definitely looks like she knows her way around a bar.

"Excuse me?" the patron replies.

"I just saw you ask a therapist, a mentor, and a coach for drink recommendations. You forgot the *real* expert in the room." She points to herself. "The one who serves the drinks."

The patron turns to the coach with a questioning look.

The coach shrugs. "She's got a point."

All right, I'll admit that analogy – or questionably bad 'walks into a bar' joke – went a little off the rails at the end. But do you get my point? Coaching is so much more empowering than therapy because every action you take is totally your choice.

2

COACHING? WHAT'S THAT?

Every move you make is *your* decision.

Let's talk about business coaching for a moment. While we do sometimes need to put our trainer hats on and teach people what we know – or share a metaphor or story to guide someone to make their own decision – coaching is all about asking kick-ass questions. Putting people in boxes doesn't get the best results. Period. Email marketing worked for one person? Doesn't mean it will work for someone else. Paying for advertising helped the million-dollar business get clients? Doesn't mean it's good for the business doing five figures that hasn't quite nailed its niche and messaging yet. Face-to-face coaching was effective for some? Doesn't mean it's right for others. One particular social media platform helped someone get more clients? Doesn't mean it's ideal for everyone. You get my point.

Don't listen to what everyone else is telling you to do and blindly follow their advice, especially if they are marketing to you. No matter your niche, no matter the service you offer, marketing a business should always be about asking the right questions, building rapport and trust, keeping the conversation going, and tailoring a strategy that suits not only the person right there in front of you – your next client – but also YOU. After all, it's your business, right? It's what makes providing a service so fun, fulfilling, and impactful. So, watch, learn, and find someone who will help you craft a strategy that works for you. Don't ignore the other experts in the room. Sometimes the bartender knows best.

Forgive the minor detour – okay, it was a major reroute. But this is a journey, and my thoughts on coaching are all a part of the trip. Now where was I? *Ahem*. It wasn't long before I found my ideal coach. See, we're back on track already.

I discovered a coach who was living in Bali, working three days a week, and running retreats in different parts of the world so people would pay him to travel. How could I not be inspired by that? I could see myself living similarly. Better mental health, a career that would give me comfortable earnings, the ability to travel – *freedom.* It doesn't get much better than that. How did I find him? Your first marketing lesson – be vulnerable. I wanted someone who I could connect with, who would understand me and what I was going through, so I went over to Uncle Google and typed 'gay coach' into the search bar. Three results came up, and he was one of them. *Three results*. Globally, for gay coaches, in this day and age? I was shocked, but, hey, he had found a niche market. He wasn't hiding, and it landed him a client.

Do you see now the importance of putting yourself out there and sharing your story? It's not just about your tools or even your results. People want to connect with *you,* the real you. That means presenting your authentic, vulnerable self to the world. You *do not* need to look perfect. In fact, it's the exact opposite. When you put yourself out there, you don't just attract more clients; you attract the *right* clients, the people who resonate with you and your message. That's who you want to be helping, right? Show people who you are, and you'll attract your ideal client like bees to honey. Are bees even attracted to honey? I don't know. Bears to honey? That sounds better. Your ideal clients will come at you like hungry bears, in the best possible way.

As a coach, I'm a big believer that if I think my clients need a coach, then I need to practise what I preach. So, I always have a coach myself. One of my coaches was based in Spain, so I had to jump on calls at mega weird times. Like,

4 am type times. But I made it work. You might be asking, "Why didn't you just find a coach in a more compatible time zone?" Great question. I did *a lot* of research while searching for my ideal match. But we had the connection, and he had the tools I needed. If someone clicks with you and your message, they'll go out of their way to work with you. Your services will practically sell themselves. Remember this. Share your story. Share *yourself*.

Finding the right coach was a huge turning point for me, as it is for many people. It completely changed the trajectory of my life in the most amazing way. After experiencing coaching, I knew I had stumbled upon something special, and I was on the verge of making a life-changing decision.

Coaching was everything I loved about my previous leadership roles: asking powerful questions, helping people grow, and guiding them through difficult situations. From a business perspective, I loved the idea of helping people improve their systems, craft their brands, and grow their revenue. Not only had I found the help I needed to move forward in my life, but I had also stumbled upon my dream career. As a coach, I could have the freedom I wanted and create the impact I desired, all while doing something I loved. Every. Single. Day. After months of lying in bed, acting as if the solution was at the end of the next video game, I had finally found a clear path forward. Coaching was my ideal career.

MY FIRST BUSINESS BOMBED IN A BIG WAY

Before I considered coaching as a career, I picked up some work driving Uber. I actually loved the job, mainly because I was no longer working in corporate, and I spent my whole day discovering new places and talking to new people. Granted, I was lucky to make more than $200 a day, but I was free to work whenever and as much as I wanted. I was practically my own boss – and it felt great!

I also started a few businesses that totally bombed. Don't think for a second that I was an overnight success. Getting to where I am today took a lot of failing forward. Every business that blew up in my face was a learning opportunity. Each time, I learnt what worked and what definitely didn't. Every failure brought me one step closer to success. Thankfully, too, because there were a lot of failures. Your failures can propel you forward faster than anything else. Are you embracing yours? There is no such thing as taking one step forward and two steps back, because you are always learning and growing.

With the help of my coach, I figured out what I wanted in a job. I wanted location freedom; I wanted to set my own hours, and I, of course, wanted to love what I did. No more dread when waking up on a workday, no more hitting the snooze button 15 times. I knew I needed to build something myself so I wouldn't hit that brick wall again. I wanted the freedom to grow, to really move the dial, and to create a massive impact in the world.

Before I decided to become a coach, I was looking into anything I could do as a work-from-home job. I even applied for copywriting and graphic design work, even though I had no formal training in these areas. I wasn't faking it. Not exactly. I knew I could write well, and I was pretty handy with a few graphic design apps, so I decided to go with it. I also considered selling supplements online. However, none of these ideas really got off the ground.

2

My biggest venture – and one of my greatest failures – was an online art and homewares business. The idea was to manage retail sales for local artists and furniture designers. I put a lot of effort into this one, signing up some good artists and building a slick, new website. If you build it, they will come, right? Wrong. So wrong. As you might know – and I know now – there's a lot more to it than that. I soon learnt that simply **building a website doesn't make customers magically appear and start spending money**. Who'd have thought? I had neglected to consider promotion and marketing *at all*. Learning the art of online advertising, which is second nature to me now, was too much for me at the time, so the business bombed. I am, however, grateful for that failure because I learnt a lot about entering the online space, which is what I needed when I finally became a coach.

FROM CORPORATE DRONE TO ASPIRING COACH

I was never going to be satisfied in corporate, no matter which rung of the ladder I reached. I had been there, done that, and learnt a valuable lesson about what my ideal life *doesn't* look like. As shattering as the abrupt end to my corporate career was, I needed to have that experience and overcome it to get to where I am now. I wouldn't take it back for anything.

I toyed with the idea of becoming a coach for some time before I finally took the plunge. I loved having conversations with my coach, not just because of the value he provided but also because of how he communicated with me. The conversations we had were like those I used to have with my team. For me, being a leader is about helping others and seeing them succeed and grow. Funnily enough, that's also what being a coach is about. You can probably see why the career appealed to me. Okay, I'll admit that the idea of only working three days a week, making a good income, and running retreats all over the world was also appealing. Let's not understate the perks. As a coach, I could earn four times my corporate salary, and I wouldn't have to work 80 hours a week. Dream job, right? Nope. *Better*. Because it wasn't a dream. It was something I knew I could do, and do well. A career in coaching was one-hundred-percent real and totally achievable. I just had to go for it.

Unfortunately, I was hesitant to take the leap. Yes, I had finally found my ideal career. But what if it became just another failed venture? What if I wasn't good enough? What if no one wanted to work with me? What if? What if? What if? Self-doubt and uncertainty can cripple the best of us. Mindset is everything. That's why a big part of the Level Up Formula focuses on this massive hurdle that many entrepreneurs face. Once you learn to master your own thoughts, the possibilities are limitless. I couldn't put coaching off forever. I knew it. My coach knew it. Everyone around me knew it. Finally, my coach suggested it was time to make a decision, and that was the push I needed.

Once I committed to pursuing a coaching career, I put time and effort into finding the right course. Sure, I could've woken up the next day, called myself a life coach, and started coaching right there and then. It certainly would have been the easiest route. But was it the best? Absolutely not. If I was going to do this, I wanted to do it right. So, I asked the question: "How do I become

> **A picture is worth a thousand words, but the way I paint I'm going to need to contact an editor.**
>
> JAMES LEE SCHMIDT

the best coach possible?" If I wanted to be an expert in the industry, I needed the right qualifications, the right mentors, the right people around me. Eventually, I found a reputable college that offered a highly regarded master practitioner course with the widest range of accreditations. NLP. Hypnosis. Behaviour profiling. You name it; I've studied it. The program was awesome and gave me a powerful start to my coaching career. Always start strong. Build momentum early.

You'll get where you want to go much faster.

MY FIRST PAID COACHING GIG

I didn't waste any time trying to get my first client. I went for it right away. Because we learnt subjects one by one, we could start coaching almost immediately. I needed to make money fast so I could stop driving Uber and commit to coaching full-time. Once I got qualified in DISC behaviour profiling, I reached out to some of my old corporate contacts to find clients. It seemed I hadn't roamed so far from the corporate world after all. *Proceed with caution.*

When I worked in corporate, I had one boss – let's call him Tony – who was a really amazing guy. He was all about growth, and he gave me and his entire team a lot of opportunities. Unfortunately, like me, he ended up on the receiving end of a not-so-positive corporate experience, which led him to leave the business. Did I mention he had the highest position in the company, just below the CEO? Yep, and we all expected him to get the top job as soon as it was available. It was pretty much a given. So, what caused Tony to leave the company? When the CEO

2

COACHING? WHAT'S THAT?

position did become available, he, of course, went for it. But he didn't get it. Cue utter disbelief across the entire business (outside of the boardroom, that is). Nine years of service. Blood, sweat, tears. Undeniable results. Tony absolutely deserved to be the next CEO. So, what went wrong? I'm glad you asked.

It seems that one of the board members had a connection with an external candidate. *Sigh.* It's an age-old story, isn't it? But a great lesson for you! We've all heard the cliche about it not being about *what* you know but *who* you know – and it's so true. The equation is simple: connections = opportunities. Anyone who believes that corporate is a meritocracy likely hasn't been in the game long enough to witness a Tony situation. In this case, it completely changed the culture of the company. *Loyalty? Hard work? Results? What will that get us? An unapologetic stab in the back – that's what!* Why would anyone stick around waiting to become the next casualty of corporate cronyism, the next Tony? When he left, I was right out the door behind him. I'm sure a few others weren't far behind, either.

When I reached out looking for coaching clients, Tony had just started a new job, which meant he also had a brand-new team. Perfect. I explained what I did and how I could help him and his team. Sure, I had never actually coached anyone before, but I could figure out the finer details once I had landed a client. How hard could it be? After our conversation, Tony signed up for a $4500, three-hour workshop. Amazing. I was only two weeks into studying to be a coach, and I had landed my first paid gig. I'd call that a roaring start. Hey, I'm well aware it's not usually – in fact, it's rarely – that easy. I was just lucky enough to have the right connections.

Because I was still driving Uber, I had to make the most of whatever free time I could find. On those cold, wet, rainy mornings, when I was working, I would purposefully drive to the airport to wait in the Uber queue because I knew I'd be sitting there for at least an hour. All the time I needed. While I waited for passengers, I would flip open my laptop and work on my coaching business. Whenever someone got into the car, I would swiftly shut my laptop, slide it down beside the driver's seat, and be ready to drive off, leaving my passengers none the wiser that I was living a double life. Yep, I was practically a secret agent at that point.

All up, I drove Uber for around three months before I fully replaced my income and transitioned to coaching full-time. Technically, I started my coaching business in my parents' granny flat, but, for a while, I was also running it from the Uber queue at the airport. Hey, I did what I had to do.

HOW I FOUND (OR DIDN'T FIND) MY NICHE

Initially, I was running a mindset coaching business for fitness professionals. It seemed like the logical place to start because the fitness industry was where I had come from, where my experience was. I began mentoring gym owners, their teams, and their members. That's where the business really started to take off. What did I learn during this time? Just get out there. Start. Explore different niches. Eventually, you'll find exactly where you fit into the industry. Don't be afraid of change. Don't hesitate to explore other options. Don't be scared to try something

2

COACHING? WHAT'S THAT?

new. I changed my niche over and over again before I found the right one. Don't think this is a business I came up with overnight. It's not. Getting to this point took a lot of trial and error, and I learnt many hard lessons along the way. I coached gym owners. I did general life coaching. At one point, I even wanted to help people with addiction. Do you see the problem there? I didn't, at first. But I quickly learnt that addicts don't generally have a lot of money. Why? Because they spend it all on drugs. That particular business concept was never going to work.

I was doing well in the fitness niche, making around $100k per year. However, I soon realised that I had fallen into an unforeseen trap. Although working with gym owners was fantastic, most of them didn't want me as just a coach. They wanted me in their businesses, fixing their operations manuals, training their sales teams, helping with compliance. Because I'm so giving, I just went with it. They were paying me a coach's wage but treating me like a consultant. It was like I was back in corporate again. The alarm bells were ringing. Something had to change. That's when I made my next big pivot.

A lot of people from the coaching college I studied at were asking me for support because they had heard about my success. They needed help finding clients, building and growing their businesses, and pretty much everything else related to running a successful coaching business. *Hmm... was there something here?* I had never considered coaching coaches before, but I seemed to have stumbled upon a big gap in the market. I understood the main problem all too well. Many of the business and marketing courses I did were too cookie-cutter. It goes back to the business mentor in the 'walks into a bar' analogy.

"Build your business this way."

"Why?"

"Because I did, and I'm successful."

"Great!"

But often, the niche, industry, audience, and many other aspects of the business are totally different. Therefore, what works for one person doesn't work for another. That's why, when I designed the Level Up Formula, I distilled a whole bunch of different courses onto one platform. Cookie-cutter doesn't actually cut the cookie. Not when it comes to building a business. I knew I had to create something different. So, at Level Up, we tailor our approach to our clients' needs. We design strategies based on how they want their lives to look. We also work out the best way for *them* to find clients instead of simply regurgitating what works for us. Remember, you're an individual. Your business should be just as distinct. You can't do it like everyone else. Instead, you need to find what works for *you* and *your business*. I learnt this early on. Now I help others know it too.

So, in the end, my niche found me.

EVERYTHING LED ME TO THIS POINT

When I first switched to coaching coaches, I thought I had made a terrible mistake – and for good reason. I ran a webinar that I was really excited about, but only one person showed up. Can you imagine my disappointment? Perhaps you've even been there yourself. It's not uncommon when first starting out. On a positive note, that one person did sign up to work with me – so it was a win overall. For anyone who runs an event and has no one show up, it's a terrible feeling. However, I ran another webinar a month later and got ten new clients. My momentum was building.

Before long, I had a healthy client list and a full schedule. Sounds great, right? Ah, but you should know by now there's always a catch. When we coach, we give a lot to our clients. We hold space for them. We give them so much energy and attention. So, when we try to squeeze too many sessions into a week, we risk leaving nothing for ourselves. Seeing 15-20 clients per week, I hit a massive roadblock. I was back in burnout mode, but this time was different. What was so different? *Everything.* Most importantly, I was my own boss, and I had the power to make real changes.

Basically, I had two options: I could either increase my prices and risk pricing out my market, or I could introduce a group format. The decision was simple. Group coaching was the answer. To help with the transition, I got my first business coach, jumping in at $3500 per month, barely covered by what I was earning at that stage. It scared the shit out of me. But I knew I worked well in high-pressure situations, and dropping a large sum of cash on a coaching program would force me to make the most of it.

With group coaching, I could impact more people in a shorter amount of time. It really was a game changer. Not just for me, but also for the coaches who I've since helped make the switch. By helping others impact more people, *I* impact more people. It's the why behind everything I do.

Another game changer for me was finding a business mentor, someone who specialised in growing online businesses. Because I had previous sales and marketing experience, I thought I knew it all. How naive I was! As it turned out, I had entered unknown territory, and I needed my business mentor to help navigate the new terrain. With my mentor's help, I went from $5-10k to $20-30k per month in a fairly short amount of time. Successful people simply don't do it alone. However, like with anything, finding the right fit is crucial.

Once I committed to group coaching, my business really kicked off, and things haven't slowed down since. Although the path I took was far from linear – it certainly had its share of twists, turns, successes, failures, and utter catastrophes – I wouldn't be where I am today if I had done anything differently. In a way, I had been preparing for a career coaching people to create their freedom-based businesses my entire life. I was a performer, remember? So, I'm not just comfortable being on stage – I fricking love it! And after working for giant companies, building and growing multi-million-dollar businesses, and managing multiple teams and hundreds of people, doing my own thing feels effortless. Most of the time. Sure, there will always be challenges, but I'm truly in my element now, and I couldn't be happier with the direction we're heading. I did the work, explored multiple niches, and, eventually, my audience found me. The journey wasn't easy, but it was well worth the reward.

I want to give a shout-out to the trail of failed ventures I left in my wake. Without those failures, I never would have learnt everything I needed to make Level Up a success. Often, we must fail today so we can succeed tomorrow. If you learn from each and every failure on your journey to success, looking back, you'll see nothing but wins. This is the mindset of a successful entrepreneur. And mindset is everything.

PART 2
MINDSET

When it comes to building a successful business, what do you think holds most people back? Lack of knowledge or skills? Low capital? No time to work on the business? Nope, nope, and nope. The biggest barrier to success for around 90 percent of the people I work with is *mindset*. That's it. Their own thoughts get in the way of them killing it in the industry. It really is that simple.

Am I good enough? Will anyone want to work with me? Can I charge this much? These are all questions that little voice, that negative Nancy in our heads, likes to ask. If your name is Nancy, I apologise. I'm sure you're a really positive person. No diss intended. But all this negative self-talk can seriously impede our growth and progress. Do you think it goes away when we achieve success? Nope. I know six- and seven-figure entrepreneurs who still question whether they're good enough, refining their target market, adjusting their products and packages. Success isn't the cure. You have to do the work and understand that how you react to those voices defines the path you carve. Again, you have to do the work, not just on your business, but on *yourself* too. In fact, cultivating a positive mindset is paramount. Focusing on the negative self-talk and limiting beliefs the little survival part of your brain has concocted will only hold you back. An unproductive mindset will stunt your success. It will stop you from reaching your full potential. Mindset matters most. Got it? Great! Let's get to work on crafting the most positive mindset on the block so you can streamline your success. Are you with me?

Chapter 3
THE BIGGEST BARRIER TO SUCCESS

A lack of skill, knowledge, and effort are the biggest barriers to success

CRAFTING THE ENTREPRENEURIAL MINDSET

While I was completing my coaching course, I met so many amazing coaches who gave me massive transformations, but they never got their businesses off the ground. Why? You guessed it: *mindset*.

It came as a bit of a shock to me. I mean, c'mon; coaches are in THE business of helping people with their mindsets. The thing is, just like anyone, we are great at giving advice and supporting others, but dealing with our own stuff can often come as a challenge if we're always trying to do it on our own. Being stuck, not feeling good enough, and procrastination galore all held them back.

Perhaps you're experiencing the same barriers right now. What do you think these people did when things got too hard? They quit coaching. They went back to the full-time jobs they hated. They gave up on their dreams. I'm here to tell you that doesn't need to be you. Each and every one of those amazing entrepreneurs had the potential to be super successful, but their mindsets got in the way. Self-care should always come first. Help yourself before you try to help others. Whatever industry you're in, when you're the face of the business, you are your brand, and being a role model for those who follow you helps them connect with you. How can we expect our clients to do the work we aren't willing to do ourselves?

Now, I'm not saying, by any means, we need to be perfect and have all our baggage resolved. In fact, it's quite the opposite. Being vulnerable and showing we are human is what connects us. Life is challenging, but that's what makes it fun.

The people who I saw abandon their entrepreneurial dreams failed to create more productive patterns. They couldn't quite craft that winning mindset they needed to keep pushing forward. So, what did they do? They leaned into their old patterns because that's where they felt safe. We thrive on the familiar. The comfort zone – it's a pretty cosy place, yeah? And it's difficult to leave when that little, or often loud, voice in your head is saying, *Stay! It's cold out there. You can't handle the cold. Stay here where it's safe, familiar, and warm. You'll only end up failing and coming back anyway. Why not just skip the failing part? You don't need to put yourself through that!* But failure to act is still failure. Worse, even. Because it doesn't move you forward. Instead, it keeps you stuck, stranded in the exact same place. Is that what we want? Hell no. We're entrepreneurs. We chase success. We don't wait for it to find us. Because it won't. As nice as it would be, it just doesn't work that way.

Don't give in to the *what if*s and *I can't*s. I'm sure you've got a few bouncing around inside your head right now. But they're meaningless. They really are. The *what if*s haven't happened yet, and *I can't*s rarely have any evidence to back them up. Agreed? Now, I want to make something clear: I'm not saying you should never consider the *what if*s, especially when it comes to legal and ethical responsibilities. But if they have anything to do with people's opinions or fear of failure, they will only hold you back. Acknowledge them. Wave them goodbye. Then toss them away. *What if people don't like my service? What if my business doesn't make enough money? What if I'm not the right person to help my clients?* Self-doubt stifles success, but it also shows that you genuinely care about what you are setting out to achieve. It means something to you, and it's okay to have a plan for *when* certain things happen, but don't expect the worst at every turn. Don't let the *what if*s hold you back. They're nothing but dead weight.

The same goes for *I can't*. You can't? Are you sure? How do you know? *I can't. I can't. I can't, I can't, I can't.* One of the best things I learnt on my journey was to treat the voice saying *I can't* like a little toddler in your head. If a toddler was standing there saying "I can't, I can't, I can't," what would you say to them? Remember this the next time an *I can't* pops into your head. That voice is just a toddler, screaming in the middle of a shopping centre, full nuclear tantrum kind of screaming. They don't know any better. So, what will you do? Whatever it takes, right?

I see *I can't* as another challenge, a chance to step up and prove my inner toddler wrong. You can do the same. Become aware of what you're telling yourself. Start to break those patterns. Imagine what you could achieve when every *I can't* becomes fuel for progress and success. You'll be unstoppable. The more you practise and adopt this mindset, the more successful you'll be – I promise you.

BE, DO, HAVE

You might already know the concept of *be, do, have.* It's a popular coaching tool. It's popular for a reason: it works. Be, do, have is based on the concept of 'fake it till you make it,' but I prefer the former. Because you're not faking it. You *are* it, right? *Right?* Some people take a little more convincing than others. I hereby declare this a self-doubt-free zone. No self-doubt allowed. Period.

Okay, so the concept of be, do, have works like this:

Be who you want to be.
Do what they would do.
Have what you want to have.

Having a vision is important. You should know what you want your life and business to look like. How can you achieve something if you don't know what you're trying to achieve? You can't. So, ask yourself, *What would I do if I were already that person?* – then do it. Simple, right? Not always, I know.

If you get stuck, do what I did and pick a role model. What do I mean by that? Pick someone you know, whether it's a celebrity, public speaker, colleague, friend, whoever you can use as a role model in any circumstance. What do you think their values are that led them to where they are now? Know how they would act in difficult situations when Nancy comes knocking in their head. Base your actions on theirs. Remember, you're not faking it till you make it. You already are it. Some of us just need a little help realising that.

But, Jim, my role model is a full-blown celeb, or they are now six feet under. How do I find out what their values are and how they overcame their challenges? That's the best part. It actually doesn't matter what they really were. It's what you see in them that's inside yourself that will drive you to success. Let them inspire you. Because for you to see the strength in others, it has to be within yourself, or you wouldn't be able to identify it.

YOU CAN'T MAKE EVERYONE HAPPY

Vulnerable moment, I am a recovering people-pleaser. Doing or saying something that made someone else not like me was one of the worst feelings I could possibly feel. Even if, deep down, I knew it had nothing to do with me, it would eat me up inside.

That was until I learnt that if you step into your true, authentic self and be true to your values, there's no way in hell you're going to make everyone happy. You're going to piss people off, and that's a good thing because you're being true to you. I'm sorry, but there's no way around it. Be prepared to take a little heat. Don't let the words of others cut you down. Craft a mindset that's impervious to hate. Hey, it's not easy – but it *is* possible. I've certainly received my share of hate over the years, especially as I've become more successful. At times, it *did* cut deep, but I didn't let myself bleed out. There are ways of viewing and dealing with people who may not be your biggest fans. As I'm sure you've guessed, mindset is key.

Being a business owner comes with its share of headaches, believe me. Stress and anxiety are a part of the package. We have to deal with complaints, lost contracts, cashflow issues, people who want to steal our hard work or get it all for free, and haters who are jealous of our success. You'll usually find the latter in the Wild West of the internet, particularly on social media. However, most haters can be safely ignored, as their hate is usually a reflection of them rather than something relevant to you.

I've had people who I thought were friends badmouth me when I've won awards. Yeah, it turned out they weren't true friends after all. You live; you learn. I also had a colleague jump onto a vulnerable post I put up and say I was just doing it to make money and was being inauthentic. When, really, I was opening up about some massive challenges in my life and wanting to show people that, hey, if I can be successful, you can too. Instead of coming to me privately, she just threw it out on social media. I was upset. It hurt, massively; I won't deny it. I didn't even know this woman. We were part of the same training community that thrived on supporting each other. Thankfully, one of my closest coaching mates helped me realise the problem wasn't with me. Something was likely going on in her life. Perhaps she'd had a bad day. I knew her accusations were groundless, so why let it bother me? It helped that everyone else who commented had my back and ended up having a go at her. Ah, sweet justice. Understand that you've got a community. A tribe. And do you know what? It can't include everyone. It's just not possible. At the end of the day, haters gonna hate. It's their nature.

Occasionally, clients will have genuine complaints, and these can help you learn and grow. But sometimes people just like to complain. These recreational complainers can put a lot of stress on you as a business owner when they insert themselves into your life. Who likes dealing with complaints? If you do happen to enjoy fielding complaints, that's an amazing superpower to have but not one that a lot of us share. A complaint can ruin a day *if* your mindset isn't solid. You're going to face objections. It's inevitable. Unavoidable. It's a part of doing business. How you handle it, not just physically but also mentally, makes all the difference.

"The customer is always right" is one of the worst phrases I've ever heard. The customer is *not* always right. Sometimes, they can be totally wrong. It's a marketing phrase, not a rule to live by. I'm not saying you should abuse your customers and call them colourful names when they step out of line, but, as a business owner, you don't need to take any unjustified shit. If you know you're in the right, why waste time dealing with complaints that have no substance? Feel free to cut clients loose if they aren't the right fit. It's not a fun thing to have to do, but, in the end, it's best for everyone.

Do you think that someone who complains right from the get-go is going to suddenly stop and change their ways? Sure, you might win them over, eventually. Then again, you might not. Is it worth the effort when you could be focusing on people who are excited to be working with you? If the conversation is too hard, you're not speaking to your ideal client. It's okay to move on. In many cases, it's for the best. You shouldn't need to persuade anyone to work with you. Let's be honest – if you have to do that, they're not going to get a lot out of your services. So, save both of you the trouble and cut them loose. It's not worth it, trust me.

> Life shrinks or expands in proportion to one's courage.

ANAIS NIN

A BIG SECRET TO SUCCESS

I'm going to tell you something that I find myself saying a lot. It may be a little hard to hear, but it's something you need to know. If you want to be successful – you do, right? – I can't withhold this information any longer. I can't ignore my duty of care. My duty *is* to care. I care that you live the life of your dreams. I care that you create the impact you want in the world. I care that you find all the success you could ever want. The secret to achieving that success? *Successful people don't do it alone*. Tough to hear, right? Not something a lot of budding entrepreneurs are willing to accept. But if you want to reach serious levels of success, you're going to need help.

As entrepreneurs and business owners, especially in the beginning, we often want to do everything ourselves. I totally admit I let my ego take over when I first started. That mindset, however, will stunt the growth of your business and push you towards burnout. Think of any bigwig in any industry. Anyone you look up to. Someone who has achieved undeniable success. Got someone in mind? It's okay if you don't. Let's use Tony Robbins as an example. Do you think that Tony Robbins is creating all of his programs by himself? Of course not! People like him – successful people, that is – know where to best direct their energy. If someone else can do the job, let them do it. Outsource. Hire a team. Do whatever you need to do so you can focus on doing what you do best. Tony Robbins is an amazing speaker, but I wouldn't be surprised if he has someone writing some of his speeches for him. If it frees him up to focus on more important things, why not? While you may not be at that level yet, I want you to start *thinking* at that level. It'll help you get there a lot quicker.

You have some amazing communities around you. Tap

into those networks. Ask for help when you need it. Don't be afraid to step aside and let someone else handle certain tasks. When I first started coaching, I made a big mistake. I was too headstrong. I wanted to figure everything out on my own, but that mindset held me back and stunted my growth. How can you learn faster? Learn from those who have come before you. If I'd swallowed my pride and got a good mentor sooner, I wouldn't have wasted so much time doing things I didn't need to be doing. It wasn't just time I wasted. I also wasted a lot of money. Time *is* money, yeah? Cliche, but true. Some tasks that took me months to complete, someone else – an expert – could have completed in a week. You can't learn everything. You can't *do* everything. Remember, successful people don't do it alone.

When you have a coach, you've committed to not doing it alone. However, you do need to maximise the *opportunity* on your own. A coach is there to guide you. They won't do all the heavy lifting. Unless you're ready to step out of your business completely, you still need to do the work.

CELEBRATE YOUR WINS AND SHARE THE HOWS

How often do you celebrate your wins? Daily? Weekly? Monthly? Yearly? Never? Celebrating our wins is so important. Why chase success if we're not going to stop and enjoy it? At the very least, you should take a moment every single week to celebrate what you've achieved and recognise how you did it. Celebrate the *what,* recognise the *how*. The how is important. Not just to help you replicate your wins, but also to help others replicate them too. We're all in this together!

3

THE BIGGEST BARRIER TO SUCCESS

I love it when people celebrate their wins publicly because it motivates everyone around them. I see it all the time in our Level Up Inner Circle group. It's like a wave. One person posts about getting a big sale, and, suddenly, more people are sharing their own big successes. How does sharing your wins help others? I'm glad you asked. It pushes people. They see what's possible, and they realise they can do it too. On top of that, if you also share the *how,* the same methods you used might work for others. Why not give someone else a chance at success? Success isn't a finite resource – so share it around!

Back when I was driving Uber, I picked up a woman, and we started talking. She asked me how I got into Uber, and I responded by practically telling her my life story. Hey, it was a long drive. What else was I supposed to do? We discussed all the stuff I had done: performed for several years in Japan; completed a BA, MBA, and now my masters; and climbed the corporate ladder to some solid success.

At the end of my spiel, she asked a single question: "How old are you?"

I was 31 at the time. "I'm thirty-one," I responded.

She turned to me. "Thirty-one? Wow, you've done so much."

When I thought about it, she was right. Compared to the average Joe, I've accomplished a lot. But, until that moment, I'd never taken stock of everything I had done and how far I had come. I realised then how grateful I was, even though I was still driving Uber. At a time when I was uncertain about the future, taking a moment to stop and recognise what I had accomplished helped shift my mindset into a more positive place. Celebrate your latest wins. Push forward to future success. But don't forget your past achievements (or failures, for that matter). They made you who you are today.

Chapter 4
MONEY MINDSET

High prices = fewer clients

Debunked!

MONEY KEEPS THE WHEELS TURNING

Money is a resource. It's not my driver. For some people, it is, and that's totally okay. But if you're on the opposite side and truly believe you aren't in business-building mode to generate a profit, then start a charity. If you don't have money, you don't have a business. Unsurprisingly, working for free isn't a great business model. You need to have a money-making goal. What's going to make you money *right now*?

Because that's the purpose of a business, right? To make money. Sure, you may also want to help people and create impact in the world. But can you really do those things if you're not making money? Perhaps. But you won't be as effective. You won't have a service that people truly value. Let's keep the math simple. A price tag equals value. A higher price tag equals greater value and doesn't necessarily mean more time or effort from you. See, what you need to focus on when it comes to creating offers is the value of the transformation, the end result someone obtains when they work with you or buy your product. It really is a simple equation.

THE DAY I DOUBLED MY PRICES (AND GOT AWAY WITH IT!)

My first mentor said to me, "Once you've sold three people at the same price, increase the price." It was good advice, but advice I was hesitant to take. Pricing was a major block for me. All I wanted to do was help people! My coach got me through it though, in a *big* way.

I was on a call with my coach, and we were discussing the four sales calls I had booked for later that day. Then he said one of the most outrageous things I'd ever heard: "Just for fun, why don't we double your price?"

"*What?*" I shat myself (figuratively). In my mind, I was about to blow four strategy sessions and lose four potential clients. I was charging around $3,000 at the time. It seemed like a lot to lose. But really, it was only four strategy sessions. *Why not roll the dice and see what happens?* So, I agreed.

I went into those strategy sessions with doubled prices, and three out of four people signed up. I couldn't believe it! A $9,000 day became an $18,000 day purely out of backing myself and the value I gave to my customers.

This was a big turning point for me regarding my money mindset. Your price, it's just a number. It's the value your clients put on the results you provide. Lowballing your price is lowballing your clients' transformations. Your service is valuable, and your pricing should reflect that.

At Level Up, we try to balance pricing with what our clients can realistically afford, using payment plans, incentives, and so on. We don't want to price them out or leave them struggling to pay the bills. Yes, your prices should match the value you want to give, but you should also consider what your audience can afford. Balance is key.

HOW TO INCREASE YOUR PRICES AND WHY YOU SHOULD

This may sound crazy, but it's easier to sell a $5,000 coaching program than it is to sell a $50 session. I'm serious. How can that be? I want you to consider this scenario: You go to the bottle shop to buy a bottle of wine. You see one bottle in the $2 bin and another on the shelf for $80. You don't know anything about the brands or actual quality of the wines, so, based on price alone, which one do you think you'll enjoy more? The more expensive one, right? Surely, the bottle with the higher price tag must be better than the one that only costs $2. It's the only logical conclusion! But it's not logical, not really. You know nothing about the two wines, so you automatically *assume* the value matches the price. The facts don't matter. You don't know the facts. You just know that price = quality. Or you *think* you know.

Guess what? Your clients and customers are doing

the exact same thing when they look at your products and services. If you're selling sessions for $50, they might agree that it's a good price. But are they really invested in it? At such a low price, it looks like you might not be experienced. Can you give them the transformation they want? The low price creates uncertainty.

When you increase your prices, you're showing your value, your confidence in what you have to offer. You're telling people that what you're offering *is* valuable. Transformative. You get results. That's what will excite them. That's what will help them understand your worth. That's what will get them scrambling to buy. Charge more money, get more clients. It sounds counterintuitive, yeah? Try it. See what happens. I think you'll be pleasantly surprised.

When it comes to raising prices, the time to do it is *now.* The world is evolving, and people are building longer and longer-term relationships with brands they trust. It really is a great time to be growing a business. In the past in the coaching world, as an example, three-month programs used to be the max most people were willing to buy. Now you can sell a 12-month package at a high price. What changed? People are craving connection. They're not in it for the quick fix. They want reliability and longevity. They want that ongoing transformation, yeah? One coach I know is selling a one-year coaching program for a million bucks. Yep, it's totally doable. Don't expect to make a million bucks right out of the gate, though. Getting to that point takes time, effort, and an unbeatable mindset around money.

What are your prices like now? Are you undervaluing yourself and your service? Can you charge more? Remember, not only is a higher-priced program more appealing, but people put more effort into something that's relatively expensive. I want you to think about one of the pricier things you purchased recently and the value you put behind it. Now think of something really cheap you bought and the value you put behind that. Do you see the difference? Did you even use all of the cheaper thing? Consider the cost of buying a home versus the cost of buying milk. Which do you value more, the house or the milk? If you're a big coffee drinker like me, you might say the milk, but most people will see the house as more valuable.

I want you to consider one final thing when it comes to pricing. You need to create your higher-ticket item *first*. It's how Elon Musk grew Tesla. The first car the company released was the Roadster, which had a fat $109,000 USD price tag.[1] From there, he was free to start adding lower-ticket products. The same strategy applies to your business. Create your higher-ticket item first. If you then want to add some lower-ticket offers, go for it. However, the lower-ticket offers are there to get people to jump into the higher-ticket programs. Got it? Great! Once you nail your high-ticket offer, you can leverage your time, hire a team, and create other offers to feed people into the high tier.

Once you get your money mindset right, you're ready to start growing and scaling your business, creating a real impact in the world, and, of course, making a healthy profit. Essentially, you're ready to Level Up and start winning in a big way.

---

[1] Gregersen, E 2022, *Tesla, Inc.*, article, Britannica, viewed 13 October 2022, https://www.britannica.com/topic/Tesla-Motors.

Chapter 5

BLUEPRINT FOR AN UNSTOPPABLE MINDSET (TIPS, TRICKS AND STRATEGIES)

Successful people wear suits

Debunked!

MINDSET MAINTENANCE

You hopefully now understand why having an unstoppable mindset is critical to success, but often it's a case of easier said than done. Overcome one challenge, and life presents you with another. This is what makes life exciting; we constantly strive to grow and evolve. If we aren't growing, we're dying. An unstoppable mindset isn't something you get and then have for life. Oh, if only life were that simple. Your mindset is something you need to maintain. It requires constant care and attention. It's like a muscle: if you want it to stay strong, you need to keep training it. Otherwise, it *will* atrophy. We don't want all those hard-earned gains to vanish now, do we? Of course not!

MY OWN PERSONAL BATTLES AND MINDSET SHIFTS

What mindset snags are holding you back right now and preventing you from reaching that next goal? If your answer is "I don't have any", then let's dig a little deeper. What fears, doubts, limiting beliefs are slowing you down? With all the work I've done on my own patterns, I can shift much faster than I used to, but no one is perfect, and we don't need to be. We just need to be quick to take action and not get sucked into the negative black hole. Which is where I found myself several years ago.

During my journey, I learnt a couple of key things about myself. First, I was a militant perfectionist, which might seem like a good thing to some people. But it was holding me back, preventing me from making progress in my life and business. Once I adopted a 'progress, not perfection' mindset, everything changed. Finally, I was gaining ground and wasn't led by a need to make everything perfect. I also had to abandon the desire to make everyone happy. You can't please everyone, nor should you try. The sooner you understand this, the sooner you can start to focus on the people who matter most, and one of those people, at the top of your list, should be YOU. Don't aim for perfection. It doesn't exist. Don't try to please everyone. It's not possible. You can't be your true, authentic self and keep everyone happy. And, my friends, this is the key to everything.

When I worked in corporate, my mindset was by far the most unproductive – and downright destructive – it has ever been. Anxiety and depression were constant. I lacked the tools to deal with them. I knew there was a problem, but dealing with it was a problem within itself. I much preferred to blank out with drugs, alcohol, sex, whatever quick fix I could find and pretend my problems weren't there. I told myself I was working on it and could do it on my own when, really, if I'd had a coach to support me sooner, I could have moved forward so much faster. So, drop the ego – it's okay to ask for help. Successful people don't do it alone.

It's also important to remember that negative feelings are just in the moment. Without them, we can't feel the good ones either. Whatever the emotion, it's how we embrace it and use it to take action that matters. When I hit a bumpy patch – and I still do – I think, *Cool, I'm doing anxiety now. It will pass. To move forward, what's the next step?* Alternatively, I could say, *I'm a really anxious person.* But what am I doing then? I'm connecting my anxiety to my identity. It's not me any more than the wind that rustles the leaves is the tree. Just as the wind always passes, the anxiety always fades. You just have to find that focused place in your mind to create safe, consistent action and ride it out. If you try to fight against the fear and anxiety or let it fuel your thoughts and actions in an unproductive way, that's when you risk doing real damage. Corporate me would wholeheartedly agree.

Here's a little hack I use when life throws a problem my way. I ask myself, *Is this going to matter in a year's time?* If it isn't, there's no point worrying about it now. Try it. Whatever the problem in front of you, ask yourself if it's going to matter in a month or a year's time. Most of the time, you'll find that those big, world-shattering issues aren't so big and world-shattering after all. Now, I want to make something clear here. I'm not saying you should ignore your problems. If an issue needs addressing, address it. Sort it out. You don't want your problems stacking up around you because then that's all you'll see: walls and walls of problems. What I'm saying is that you should choose your battles wisely. Don't let them negatively affect your mental state. Is it going to matter in a year? No? Then don't dwell on it. Save that energy for more worthwhile pursuits.

As I mentioned earlier, the customer – or the client – isn't always right. They can't be. I can't be. You can't be. No one can always be right. It's not how the world works. Sometimes, you'll take on a client who turns out to be the wrong fit. If this hasn't happened to you already, it's coming. Trust me. Ideally, you would filter these people out *before* they sign up to work with you. However, sometimes an incompatible client slips through your defences.

So, what do we do? Let's say a client turns around and says to me, "Jim, I'm not getting anywhere in my business, and it's *your* fault." Have they been doing the work? Have they been implementing the process? If the answer is no, I just let them go. I've had clients who were really excited to jump into group coaching with me only to decide they want one-on-one coaching. Sometimes, they're not even interested in growing a business. Instead, they see Level Up as a magic pill that will solve all their problems without the need to take any action. Some people work in mysterious ways. Whatever their intentions, they weren't the right fit, so I cut them loose. You have to learn to let people go. If they aren't the right fit, they're likely to cause more problems later down the track. Don't waste your time. Don't waste your energy on the people who aren't doing the work. Don't let them take you for a ride. If you can, catch them early. If someone's in the too-hard basket before they become a client, imagine what they're going to be like when they do become a paying client. Is it really worth it? We give so much to our clients in terms

> **The worth of a thing is what it will bring.**
>
> ENGLISH PROVERB

of energy and value, but we need to look after ourselves first. Consider, what's best for you? Because what's best for you is ultimately what's best for your business and, in turn, your clients. It all starts with *you*. As long as you know you're delivering and giving value, you've got nothing to worry about.

When overwhelm does creep in, it's good to have someone to vent to. I'm fortunate to have an amazing team and some great friends who know how to bring me back down to earth. You need someone who you can bounce ideas off. If someone isn't available, write stuff down. Journal. Get it out of your head. Speak it into a voice recorder if you have to. Do whatever you need to do to keep moving forward.

SUCCESSFUL PEOPLE DON'T WEAR SUITS

Entrepreneurs come in many shapes and sizes. Some are knee-deep in their businesses, frequently working on the front line. Others are a few steps back, focusing on the bigger picture. Then there's all those in between. Where are you now? Where do you want to be? What does entrepreneurship look like to you?

One of my biggest values is freedom. Freedom to travel. Freedom to take weekends off. Freedom to jump off a call and then take the dog for a walk if that's what I feel like doing. Freedom to take my lunch break whenever I want. That's why I designed my business the way I did. I wanted absolute freedom – or as close as anyone can get. Yes, I guess I'm a little scarred from my corporate experience, where freedom wasn't a part of the package. But I'm more than making up for it now because it's important to me. What do you value? What type of entrepreneur do you want to be? Do you, like me, only want to work a few days a week? Or do you want to spend every waking moment working on your business? Freedom is my value. It doesn't have to be yours. As an entrepreneur, you don't have to stick to a conventional 9 to 5 working schedule. *You* set the schedule. *You* make the rules. *You* decide what you focus on, who you work with, and what you wear. That's freedom right there.

Steve Jobs was a notorious underdresser (by corporate standards, not mine). Do you remember what he used to wear? Black turtleneck, blue jeans, white trainers. He practically had his own uniform, and he never wore a suit. In fact, when AT&T asked him to wear a suit to a meeting, an Apple rep responded with, "We're Apple. We don't wear suits. We don't even own suits."[2] The thing is, successful people don't wear suits. Sounds counterintuitive, right? In the corporate world, suits are a sign of success. But I'm not talking about corporate. That's a different – and debatable – form of success. I'm talking about the world of entrepreneurship, where the most successful people in their industries aren't slipping into a suit every morning. Often, they're dressed as casually as any random person you might meet on the street. And there's wisdom in that.

As a corporate boy, I hated getting into a suit every single day. It wasn't my style. But I was in a corporate role, so I had to wear the corporate costume. The truth is, if you are successful, you don't need to put on a suit to prove it.

---

2 Yarow, J 2010, *"We're Apple. We Don't Wear Suits. We Don't Even Own Suits"*, article, Business Insider, viewed 13 October 2022, https://www.businessinsider.com/steve-jobs-were-apple-we-dont-wear-suits-we-dont-even-own-suits-2010-7.

In fact, you may look like you're trying too hard to play a part rather than actually being the part. "What if I like wearing a suit?" I can hear some of you asking. Then wear a suit. If the authentic version of you wants to wear a suit, or a big golden chain, or a cowboy hat, then that's what you should wear. As long as you're being true to yourself, who cares? But when you're forcing yourself to put on a suit every day to impress others – like I did for so many years – you're not being authentic. You're not embracing the real you. You're not really dressing for success. You're dressing for what you – and, admittedly, many others – think success looks like. But it's an outdated image that doesn't hold up in the modern world.

When entrepreneurs – like Steve Jobs and Mark Zuckerberg – wear the same outfit every day, they're trying to reduce what's known as decision fatigue. Making decisions uses mental energy. If you can reduce the number of choices you make in a day, the theory is that you'll have more energy to spend on other tasks. Does it work? I think so, yeah. As an entrepreneur and business owner, you're making decisions every day. You don't need to be thinking about what to wear.

In my experience, cutting out that one seemingly simple decision in the morning makes managing the rest of the day a lot easier. Me? I'm usually in a plain black or white T-shirt up top and jeans or tracksuit pants down low because that's my entire wardrobe. I keep it simple. Sure, it's not very exciting, but it means I'm never stalled in the morning, trying to decide what to wear. I've got much bigger decisions to make. Why waste energy picking out clothes? I suspect that not everyone's going to be with me on this, and that's fine. If you do what best aligns with your true, authentic self, you can't go wrong.

5

REINVENTING THE WHEEL

You may be familiar with a tool called the Wheel of Life – no, not the epic board game you might have played as a kid. If you aren't, you're about to be. I've reinvented the wheel. Actually, I've split it in two: the Life Wheel and the Profit Wheel. Not so much a reinvention but more of a reimagining. I truly believe that for your business to be successful, you need to be accomplishing things in your personal life too. Otherwise, personal life interferes with business life. That's why we provide support in so many different ways at Level Up. We want people to get results in *all* areas of their lives. That's what true success looks like.

The Unstoppable Wheel is great for creating a targeted plan to help get those all-round results. Fill out each segment, see where you stand, and then you'll know exactly what you need to focus on. Simple, right? Let's get to work!

Worksheet

When running a business, it's just as important to understand where you're at personally as it is to know where you're at professionally. Looking at each of the areas below, score yourself by drawing a line through each quadrant, inside the circle being 0 (low satisfaction), outside being 10 (high satisfaction).

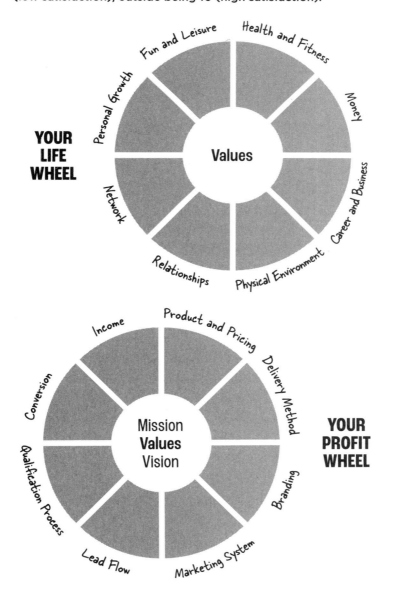

5

CHECK YOUR PRIORITIES

Looking at those wheels, are you in for a bumpy ride? Or are things running smoothly right now? To pump up those tyres, it's time to go deeper. What are your priorities? A simple question, but not one that's always easy to answer. While we often know what we *should* prioritise, our actual priorities don't always reflect this. I want you to examine your current priorities. The easiest way to do this is to look at your calendar. The beautiful thing is that your calendar can't lie. Whether your business is a side hustle or a full-time gig, just a quick glance at your schedule will reveal exactly what you're prioritising in your life right now.

So, what do you see? Are you spending a lot of time working a separate job and not much in your own business? Are you scheduling less time with family and friends than you would like? Are you filling your schedule with work and not adding in any me time? You're an entrepreneur. You are, right? You wouldn't be reading this book if you didn't have at least a spark of that entrepreneurial mindset. Remember, you get to make the rules. You get to set your priorities. I'm not saying you should go ahead and quit your full-time job. Not if the time isn't right. But you can start to shape your schedule into something that better aligns with your ultimate vision for yourself, your life, and your business. Once you have your priorities in order, your schedule will work *with* you and not against you on your journey to success. Doesn't that sound great?

> ## Action
>
> Look at your future self, let's say in three years' time, and the vision of the life you want to create. Now list, in order, the top five priorities that future you has. For example, it might be:
> 1. Self
> 2. Family
> 3. Friends
> 4. My own business
> 5. Health
>
> Now look at your current calendar and list your current priorities based on the amount of time you spend in each area right now. Do the future you and current you match? Now start identifying what you can move around to make that future you a reality. Finally, enjoy a faster path to your goals.

PROGRESS, NOT PERFECTION

I mentioned that I'm a recovering perfectionist. It's a battle that took place in my mind every day: the fight between progress and perfection. Perfection sounds great, right? Who doesn't want something to be perfect? Striving for perfection should be a noble goal. It's okay to want to do things well, but chasing perfection will only stunt your progress. What I mean is that you need to make sure you're constantly moving forward and not stalling while trying to make everything perfect. You could spend the rest of your life perfecting a product, your high-ticket offer, messaging, whatever it is and never get there. Why? Because perfection is a myth. It doesn't exist. Often, good enough really is good enough. It has to be. I know the perfectionists among us will shake their heads at that. My inner perfectionist is doing some head shaking right now. But perfection is poison to progress. Period. While you're making tiny changes, trying to see how perfect you can make a thing, your business can't grow. Not at a decent speed, anyway.

If you're a perfectionist – hello, friend! – I want you to start focusing on progress over perfection. Remember, you set the expectations much higher on yourself than those around you do. Focus on getting stuff done. Just get it out there. You can tweak, change, edit it later, but you want to move towards your goal as quickly as possible. Consider your goal – what is it? It could be growing your business to six or seven figures per month, gaining more clients, getting more traction – all that jazz. Whatever your goal is, trying to make everything perfect will only slow you down. Your primary focus should be moving forward.

As a somewhat recovered perfectionist, I can say that the key to overcoming perfectionism is examining the way you view failure. Take a leaf out of my book (that would be *this* book): I don't believe that failure is going backwards. It actually moves you forward. Crazy, right? Unlike perfection, failure *is* progress. It's all about failing forward. Don't be afraid to fail. Embrace your failures. They are just moving you towards your next success. Come in with that mindset, and the pattern of perfectionism is a lot easier to break. If you try something and it doesn't work, learn, move on, and don't do it again. Or do it differently. Whatever fits the situation.

I'm not saying you shouldn't try to do things well. However, perfectionism that stems from fear of failure isn't productive. It's a progress killer. Remember, failure is your friend. That doesn't mean go out there and *try* to fail, but failure's nothing to fear. It's a learning opportunity that helps you and your business grow. So, get out there and start failing!

THE ONLY WAY TO BUILD CONFIDENCE

Do you want to know a little secret? Absolute confidence is unachievable, even when you're the king of the hill. Why? Because there are always new things you need to become confident in. We must understand that confidence isn't something that magically appears one day. Confidence comes when you achieve something. So, if you're sitting around waiting to feel confident about something *before* you do it, I'm sorry to tell you, but that day may never come. You can't build confidence without first doing the thing. It doesn't come before. It's an after-effect, something you earn by doing the work, taking the leap, and stepping out of your comfort zone.

Is there something important you're waiting to feel confident about? Perhaps you don't feel confident about starting group coaching or scaling your business. Whatever it is, don't wait. Go ahead and do it anyway. See what happens. I promise you that confidence will come quicker the more you decide to expand your comfort zone. If you want to be super successful, a small, curated comfort zone just won't cut it. You've got to make room for confidence, yeah? Confidence comes from doing the things you don't feel confident doing.

Action

Go out and do one thing you're not confident in.
Repeat this activity as often as possible.
Watch your confidence boom!

ACKNOWLEDGE YOUR FEARS

When you shoot for the stars – which is what all of us should be doing – some fears are going to come up. Don't ignore them. Don't try to bury them deep inside. Instead, openly acknowledge them. What are your fears? Fear of failure? Fear of success? Fear of balloons (globophobia)? That's a tough one to deal with at party time. Acknowledging your fears is the first step. The next is to overcome them.

Action

List your top four fears.
Write down what you're going to do to overcome them.
Set a due date to start each action you've created.
Put them into your calendar and hold yourself accountable to taking those steps.
Go!

1.

2.

3.

4.

START YOUR MINDSET SHIFT NOW

When it comes to mindset, there's something you need to know: change won't happen overnight. As an entrepreneur, consistency and persistence are the keys to everything. Want to grow your business? Be consistent and persistent. Want to achieve your ideal life? Be consistent and persistent. Want to craft an unstoppable mindset? Yep, you guessed it. Be consistent and persistent. Every action, even the small ones, puts you one step closer to your goal. Some moments will be harder than others. That's business. That's life. Remember, failure is not an excuse to quit. Failure is an opportunity to learn and a reason to move forward.

If you put in the hard work now, it will pay off in the future. Without a doubt. My life coach once said to me, "The energy that you put out into the world is eventually going to come back." So, work your butt off *right now*. Six months of hard work could lead to a lifetime of success and freedom. Fair trade-off? I think so.

Build is the foundation of the Level Up Growth Strategy. However, it may not be the step that's most relevant to you. You may have already laid the foundations of your business by nailing your niche, crafting your offer, and creating a clear model for how you want your business to grow and scale. The beauty of the Level Up Formula is that you can jump to any topic at any time and focus on whatever's relevant to you and your business right now. With that said, some of the tips, tricks, strategies, and activities in the Build section may help enhance what you've already achieved. There's only one way to find out, right?

If, however, your business is still in the early stages, Build is a great place to start. Without laying the right foundations, it's difficult to take that next step, expand on what you've built, and get the results you're looking for. You want your business to be structurally sound, yeah? Lay a dodgy foundation, and you risk compromising everything you build on top of it. Instead, let's construct something solid so your business will not only survive but thrive.

Chapter 6
NAIL YOUR NICHE

You should cast your marketing net as wide as possible

NAVIGATING THE N WORD

When it comes to the N word, a lot of entrepreneurs get stuck. I am, of course, talking about *niche*. **Who** do you want to serve? **Why** do you want to serve them? **What** do you have to offer? And, most importantly, what is the **Transformation** you can give them?

The overwhelm that comes with choosing a target audience is not just a pitfall for startup business owners. I've coached million-dollar company directors on adjusting and tweaking their target market. So, for those of you in startup mode, I want to begin this section with this: your niche will never be perfect, so just choose. Try it on like a new jacket and if it doesn't fit, put it back on the rack. Just choose.

Whatever you're selling, you need to remember that a client who makes a purchase is making it for them, not for you. The key to marketing is to focus on the result they want to get when they work with you, not your qualifications, experience, time they get to spend, or the amount of stuff you want to give them. Help them see the pot of gold at the end of the rainbow.

I ask all of my clients this one question when they are stuck on choosing an audience: if the perfect person walked through the door right now and said, "I want to work with you," who are they? A good niche should be narrow. The more specific you make it, the more clients you'll get. Sounds counterintuitive, right? But a lot of business owners make the mistake of casting a wide net with their marketing. They want to catch as many clients as possible, which is totally understandable, and they think the more general they go, the more clients they'll get. However, when your net is too wide, catching your ideal client is harder.

Let's go a little further with a fishing analogy. Picture a trawler that's cruising along with a big, wide net, scooping up anything in its path. Perhaps it's trying to catch one specific type of fish, but it ends up with a whole lot of sea life of varying shapes and sizes. What happens then? The fishermen must sort through everything in the net to find their ideal fish. Not only is this a time-consuming task, but they also risk missing their ideal fish among the others. Surely, there's a better way to do it, right? Absolutely.

Whether you're new to marketing or someone who has been doing it for a while, ask yourself, "How wide is my net?" Are you targeting a specific type of person (your ideal client)? Or are you dragging up the entire contents of the ocean with your marketing? You may not even need a net at all. When you've nailed your niche and your marketing is on point, it's more like you're fishing with bait. You attract the exact client you want to work with, and all you have to do is reel them in. While a targeted approach may seem like it will hook fewer clients, you'll be hooking *the right* clients. I'm talking about the 20 percent of people who generate 80 percent of your income, the ones who are happy to pay 4 to 5 figures for what you have to offer. They are the people you want to bait your hook for. Those are the people you want to work with because you know they sincerely want to work with you. They didn't just get caught up in some overly wide marketing net. If they didn't want to work with you, they wouldn't have taken the bait. Well, most of the time at least. Sometimes fish – and clients – do make mistakes. That's why you should always inspect what's on your hook before reeling it in. Curate the room, your future self will thank you.

WHAT DO PEOPLE REALLY BUY?

As I mentioned briefly at the start of this chapter, one of the most important things to remember when nailing your niche is this: people don't buy information. They buy transformation. As much as we might like to think they do, they don't buy *you*. Yes, rapport, trust, and a story that resonates are important in attracting clients and getting them to make a purchase. However, they're not buying you or even the information you provide. The transformation is what it's all about.

In the age of the internet, information is everywhere. I could look up right now 'how to choose a niche'. What would I find? Heaps of articles written by hundreds of authors that cover a wide range of industries. Clearly, it's not information people want to buy - information is free! - it's what they'll receive from the application of the information we provide that they're willing to pay for. That is, the transformation.

Let's consider my program, Level Up. Our clients know our course will give them a transformation, a huge one, if they apply the strategies we teach them. We have the right information. We know how to help our clients apply it. But we also make sure we provide all the extras that enhance our clients' journey. Support. Accountability. Community. All of these things help facilitate transformation. *This* is what we sell. Make sure it's what you're selling too.

NAILING YOUR NICHE

Let's now go through the process of really nailing your niche. Don't think that once you've hammered in the nails you can't pull them out. Your niche can - and likely will - change and evolve over time. I know mine did. Also, remember,

> your niche is not the only audience you work with; they're simply the people you market to.

So, build rapport with the people you want to work with. Show that you understand them, where they're at, and where they want to go. If your message and marketing are right, they'll know you're the one to help them to achieve their goals. Then they're more likely to buy without hesitation. Makes sense, right? Great!

Let's get to work on nailing your niche.

Worksheet

Your niche audience is 20 percent of clients you will work with that will bring 80 percent of your income. It is not the be all and end all; it is never set in stone and is ever evolving.

Let your ideas flow onto the page, then you can edit, review, reframe as much as you like, but at least you have a starting point.

Which of these is the main focus of your niche?

Wealth   Health   Relationships

What problem do you want to solve?

_____
_____
_____
_____
_____

Who can you solve it for? (come up with as many as you like)

_____
_____
_____
_____
_____

Which are the most profitable? Who would/could pay the most?

_____
_____
_____
_____
_____

Who would get the most benefit?

_____
_____
_____
_____
_____

Based on the last three questions, who has scored the highest?

_____
_____

What would this niche google to find you?
Choose five keywords. These will be used in your marketing copy, blog posts, and so on to maximise your ranking on search results – for example, coach, fitness, leadership, wellbeing, community

_____
_____
_____
_____
_____

WORKSHEET – NAILING YOUR NICHE

CREATE YOUR IDEAL CLIENT PROFILE

All right, so we've nailed our niche as best we can. It will grow and evolve. Next, we want to create our ideal client profile. Once again, I'm not talking about the people you will work with full stop. I'm talking about that niche audience you'll target with your marketing. Who is your ideal client? Not sure? Then this activity is the perfect way to get you thinking. It's time to profile your ideal client.

Worksheet

Before we go any further, we need to understand who you are talking to. Your avatar is a visualisation of your perfect client.

Depending on what level your business is at, you might have multiple avatars. If this is the case, duplicate this page for each character you are creating.

Name _____

Age _____

Gender _____

Relationship status _____

Children _____

Location _____

Occupation _____

Education level _____

Annual income _____

Goals and Values

_____
_____
_____
_____
_____

Challenges and Pain Points

_____
_____
_____
_____
_____

Interests

_____
_____
_____
_____
_____

Online and Offline Social Activities

_____
_____
_____
_____
_____

5

NAIL YOUR NICHE

How you structure your products and services and talk to clients in your marketing will all come down to demographic and psychographic testing. For example, if your ideal client values freedom and variety, you need to structure your strategy in a way that caters to this. You can't expect to post an hour-long video about your ultimate tool for success and hold their attention. It's not what this particular client wants. They want variety, and they want it fast. If you don't give it to them, they're going to lose interest. Instead, you could break videos up into five-minute snippets. Let them complete a step on their journey with you in, say, five or ten minutes, as opposed to an hour or more. Then they get that feeling of variety. They get that feeling of quick and constant progress, ticking a box faster and easier. They also get that feeling of freedom. Why? Because they don't feel like they need to be tethered to their laptop for an hour at a time, watching videos. Some people have shorter attention spans. After being diagnosed with ADHD at age 36, I certainly relate. Good luck getting me to sit through an hour-long video if it's not engaging and action focused. But bite-sized chunks? I could devour them all day long.

Remember, this is just an example. Your ideal client may be totally different. If they're someone who can sit through the entire Lord of the Rings trilogy without a bathroom break, you could probably deliver your course as a four-hour documentary, and they'd be fine with it. In fact, they'd prefer it that way.

It all comes down to this: who do you want to work with? Yes, this is about you too. Do you want the quick action takers or the thorough, concise planners? There is no right or wrong here. But the answer tends to lie in your own traits and, in the long run, will make creating and working with your audience easier.

You must also consider your ideal client's values in your marketing. If you don't offer what they value, they're not going to value your offer. Again, let's use the example of that ideal client who wants variety and freedom (you can tell what my two highest values are, right?). If you're, for instance, in the health and wellness space, you wouldn't market a strict eating plan and fitness routine, where chicken and broccoli are all that's on the menu for every meal of every day and the exercise program is repetitive. Instead, you'd want to offer flexibility. They don't want to eat the same thing, day in, day out. As a foodie, this would be hell for me. And for many others, I'm sure. They don't want to re-enact the same fitness routine over and over like they're stuck in a time loop. Consider what your ideal client values. Create a service based on these values. Bait the hook! That is, use your marketing to make sure your ideal client knows what you're offering. Sounds obvious, yeah? But sometimes we get so caught up in explaining our tools and the amazing transformations we can provide that we neglect to focus on what the client values, whatever that may be.

As with everything, your ideal client profile doesn't have to be perfect. You can edit and update it at any time. The important thing is that you're thinking about who this person is and how you can effectively speak to them and their needs, yeah? The goal is to continue pushing forward – so let's keep moving!

NARROW YOUR NICHE

Before the real fun begins and we give your niche a good old-fashioned shakedown, I want you to reflect on the work you've already done. Do you feel like you've gained some clarity to move forward? Remember, perfection isn't the goal. At this point, we're just looking to move you closer to your ultimate goal. You can fine-tune along the way.

Also, have you nailed your ideal client? *Ahem.* Let me rephrase that. Do you feel that you understand your ideal client enough to effectively communicate your message to them and get them on board with what you have to offer? If not, that's okay. Rome wasn't built in a day, and not all niches are nailed in an afternoon. Keep working on it. You'll find that clarity comes a lot quicker than you might think.

If you think you've got your niche sorted, I've got news for you. We're going to narrow it down further. *What?* Yep, we're no longer using bait and hook. We're going spear fishing. We're targeting our ideal client as precisely as possible. Let's see how narrow we can go.

Disclaimer: please do not actually spear any clients. That's bad for business (and not so great for your clients, either). Spear them with clever marketing, not with an actual spear. Got it? Good!

When designing a product or service, we often try to come from the angle of a generalist because we want to work with as many people as possible. But that's not the best way to grow your business, nor is it the best way to help your clients. To really hit your stride in your industry, you need to specialise. Be an expert at one thing before a generalist in many things. Specialise in something awesome and provide one key puzzle piece so it's easy for your audience to understand that you have exactly what they need. That's the goal when nailing your niche.

But there's more to it than just attracting the right clients. Specialising will also help you scale. At Level Up,

> **Your niche is the ideal clients you market to, but they are not the only people you work with.**

JIM COCKS

we're really selective when it comes to who we work with. We want everyone who comes on board to work together as a tribe. It creates more value for our members but also makes our jobs easier, yeah? Our members support each other. They celebrate one another's successes. They work as a tribe, with everyone's best interests at heart. If you curate the room, you're going to create more success for your clients. Not only because you're working with the right people, but also because the right people are working together. Only working one-on-one right now? Doesn't matter. Start to curate the room now. Why? Because when you start to scale and build a community, the right people will already be there.

There was a stage in my company where I needed to fire over 45 clients. They weren't a good fit, and they weren't doing what they needed to do to succeed. Instead of holding them accountable to the actions they weren't taking, I was being way too nice, working with them for free and giving them extra support. Like pushing a huge boulder up a hill, this not only impacted my energy, but it also drastically impacted my community. Lots of bad eggs pulled all my other clients down. So, I had to have some really tough conversations. Once those conversations were had, not only did I feel a massive weight off my shoulders, but my clients started achieving more. At Level Up, we increased our prices and within just a few weeks, we had increased our monthly revenue by $40,000. How, you ask? Well, the great wins our clients were getting turned into amazing testimonials. People started referring more of their friends to us because they loved the program so much.

Don't be the nice one. Be the effective one.

So, let's talk about narrowing our niche down a little

more. Really, we're looking for the niche within the niche. What are the specific problems you could help with? While your current niche may have a lot of different issues, what's the one you love working on? Or what would you really love to help people create? For example, if you're working with athletes, maybe you want to work with aspiring Olympians. Always try to think narrower. I challenge you to seriously niche down. The more you specialise, the easier it is for your ideal client to find you. When someone has a specific problem they want solved, they're going to look for a specific person. That person might as well be you.

Action

Identify at least five niches within your niche and write them down. Can you specialise in one of these areas?

THE NICHE-NAILING CHECKLIST

I wouldn't tell you to narrow your niche without giving you the tools to do so now, would I? Of course not! Once you've identified your potential niche, the next step is to see if it can fit into a viable business model. That's where the niche checklist comes in. Once you complete it, you should have a clearer idea about whether your niche is worth pursuing and what the next steps might be. Sounds simple, right? I know that a good niche can be hard to nail down, so I'll offer a little guidance around each item on the checklist. Let's get into it.

❏ **Can I work with them now?**

Is their problem relevant right now? Or is it something that will only be an issue later down the track? For example, starting one-to-one paid coaching is a massive step for startup coaches. If I start talking to them about creating a group coaching program, overwhelm sinks in. They're not ready to work with me on this straight away.

❏ **Can I give massive value?**

Simple question, right? But super important. Can you give your niche massive value? If not, it may not be the niche for you.

❏ **Do they know they need help?**

This is of the utmost importance. Do your ideal clients actually know they need help? You don't want to be talking to people who don't think they need you. Do you really want to waste your time fighting that uphill battle? Your niche doesn't just need to have a specific problem you can solve. It also needs to *know* it has a problem that needs solving. Some people genuinely don't recognise – or aren't willing to acknowledge – that they need help. If that describes your proposed niche, they aren't ready to hear what you have to offer.

❑ Do they self-identify?

Do they self-identify with who you say you work with? For example, a lot of people who want to work with business owners say they want to work with entrepreneurs. But do those people actually identify as entrepreneurs? Coaches, trainers, therapists, business owners – they're all entrepreneurs. But is that the label they self-identify with most? In order to speak to them, you need to see them as they see themselves. This is super important.

❑ Can I speak their language?

Can you speak your niche's language? What are their values? What are the words that identify who they are and what they want to achieve? Some people might be looking for profit. Others want to create impact. Use language that connects to *their* mission, not necessarily yours. Because, hey, people prefer when it's all about them.

❑ Can they easily afford it?

The big one – can they easily afford it? There's no point trying to build a business around a niche that can't afford to pay you. Period. Unless you're running a charity of volunteers, you need revenue to sustain and grow your business. For example, I found out the hard way that people with serious addiction generally don't have a lot of money for coaching sessions. While I wanted to help those people, it wasn't a viable business model. I had to accept that and move on.

Another reason why we need to narrow our niche is because the service will seem more specialised and, therefore, more valuable. People will be willing to pay more.

❏ Do they all have the same challenges?

Is everyone in your niche facing the same problems? Yes, I know we like to think our problems are unique to us, but that's rarely the case. Generally, everyone in your niche should have the same issues. What does this mean? You can offer them the same – or similar enough – solutions. This helps a lot with scalability. While every client is unique, often their biggest problems are not.

❏ Would they benefit from a community?

No matter who you want to serve, would they benefit from being in a tribe? Community is a big part of Level Up, and it adds massive value for our members. But cultivating a supportive community would be a waste of time if our niche wouldn't benefit from it.

❏ Can I scale easily?

Finally, are you setting yourself up to create a scalable business? It's important to consider this as early as possible. Ideally, right from the start. You may not understand how to do it yet, but you should make getting to the next level as easy as possible when the time comes.

Once you've completed the checklist, write down your top takeaway and the next steps you're going to take. What could those next steps look like? Maybe you've identified your ideal niche and need to start targeting your marketing towards them (it's time to go spear fishing!). Or perhaps you need to redefine your niche because it doesn't quite fit a profitable, scalable, successful business. Whatever your next steps are, don't just write them down. Do them! I'm all about action; you may have noticed. Without action, we can't gain traction, and we want to keep moving forward, yeah? Because that's where our goals are. They're not behind us. The goals we've reached are achievements. Our current goals are always in front of us, and the only way to reach them is to keep moving forward.

Jim is sharing more in his BONUS MATERIAL.

See exclusive downloads, videos, audios and photos.

DOWNLOAD it now at clearedgecoaching.com.au/beitraining

Worksheet

- ❏ I can work with them now
- ❏ I can give massive value
- ❏ They know they need help
- ❏ They self identify
- ❏ I can speak their language
- ❏ They can easily afford it
- ❏ They all have the same challenges
- ❏ They would benefit from community
- ❏ I can scale easily

Chapter 7
CRAFT YOUR OFFER

Working with groups is less effective than one-to-one

WHAT REALLY DETERMINES WHAT CLIENTS ARE WILLING TO PAY

As business owners, we just want to help people, right? And that's great. But how much of an impact can you create when you don't have the finances to back your mission? Some, perhaps. But wouldn't you prefer to get your pricing on point and make a tidy profit if you could? Hey, if money is your primary motivator, I don't need to waste time convincing you. However, a lot of people starting out struggle to overcome the hurdle of going from cheap, or even free, services to high-ticket. When they can't bring themselves to start charging what they're worth, they devalue the service and the transformations they're providing.

So, I'll ask you, are you charging enough? Before you answer, I want to let you in on a little secret. Actually, it's a big secret that implicates almost every industry on earth. Skill and confidence are *not* connected to price. Sounds crazy, right? Surely, the more skilled, experienced and confident you are, the more you can charge. Nope. Not how it works. Have you ever worked with someone who charges an incredibly high price, and you can't quite figure out how or why? If you look around, you'll see it a lot. The answer? Great marketing. That's it. They're no more skilled than the next person. Their experience isn't anything to write home about. Their confidence - well, they must be somewhat confident if they're willing to slap a big price tag on their service, but it's not the main factor that's driving their sales. So, what's the deal?

People invest in what they think is valuable. If somebody really wants that massive transformation, they *will* pay for it. Simple as that. They'll pay a price that matches the value they have in their head. It's not about your skill, experience, or even the time you offer your clients, unless you're a relaxation massage therapist or similar, booking someone in for a 30-minute session. If they get less time than they paid for, they might feel ripped off. However, in many cases, time isn't a factor. Well, actually, it is a factor, but, generally, the faster and easier it is - not the harder and longer - the better. If you're a coach, have you ever given someone a transformation within the first 15 minutes of a session? It happens. Does the client feel ripped off if the session ends early? Hell no. They got exactly what they wanted. It's all about the transformation you're providing them. Results matter. All of that other stuff is just noise. Sell transformations, not skill or experience. Confidence is great but not totally necessary. It will build over time. When you market to your niche, transformations are what you should be selling.

If you're marketing and selling your time, I'm talking three-, six-, twelve-session packages, I want you to stop that right now. Why? I'm sure you can guess. It's not about the number of sessions it takes to get results. It's about the results themselves. A transformation could take one session, or it could take twenty. Doesn't matter. The transformation is what your clients want to buy, so that's what you need to sell. Say you're a writer, editor, or graphic designer, helping someone publish their book. Wouldn't they pay you more if you could get the job done faster?

Clarity is also really important. Have you ever looked at the menu at a restaurant only to find that it's ten pages long and you can't decide what to order? Decision overwhelm is real. When presented with too many options, we take longer to decide or, in some cases, can't decide at all. Do we want to put our clients in that position? Of course not. We want to make the entire journey as easy as possible for them. So, make sure you're providing a clear, simple product that works for them. If they haven't worked with someone in your space before, they won't know what the best option is. They won't understand half the things on the menu. Remember, you're the expert. Provide them with what you know will get them the result they want. The best restaurants have small menus or, sometimes, no menus at all. They know what they do well. They know not to overwhelm people with too many choices. Most importantly, they know what their customers need. Simplicity is key to clarity.

NAME YOUR PRICE!

Considering the transformations you know you can provide, what's your price? What are clients willing to pay for the results you help them get? If you haven't yet built confidence in this area, I don't want you to focus on what you *think* clients will pay. What are they *actually* willing to pay? Remember, nothing is set in stone. We're not building the pyramids here. Price is just a word (and a number). It can always change.

If you're unsure what to charge, experiment a bit. Get crazy with it. Keep saying prices out loud until one makes you laugh, then you've probably gone too high. Remember when I said I doubled my price and still closed three out of four sales? What I thought would ruin me – or those four potential sales at least – became an instant Level Up. Are you holding back on an opportunity to Level Up your business in a big way? Don't hold back. If your clients understand the transformations you can give them – get that marketing right! – they'll pay for the value they see.

Many of us lack confidence in this area. It's not uncommon for people who want to serve and support others to want to undercharge for their services. Yes, you don't want to price out your market, but you also don't want to devalue your service or your clients' transformations. Still lacking confidence when it comes to pricing? Let me ask you this. Are there people in your niche who charge more than you? What makes their services better? I promise it's not skill or experience. If you believe they're offering a better service, what can you do to make your service as good as, if not better than, theirs? Write it down. Create an action plan. And please, actually take action on it! Once your service rivals others that are priced higher, you'll have the confidence to charge more too.

If, however, the competition's got nothin' on you, what are you waiting for? The time to up your prices is *now*.

WORKING WITH GROUPS IS KING

Most of us start out working with people one-on-one, and we think it's the ultimate way. I'm sure you understand my position by now. Creating services where you can work with multiple people at once is king. Period. It takes up less of your precious time. It helps you impact more people. Most importantly, it creates bigger transformations for your clients. It really does take a village to help people grow. We promote and push the group format for these reasons.

- Why not do the thing that takes less time and brings in more money?

- Why not create as much impact as possible?

- Why not aim for bigger and better transformations?

Once you overcome the limiting belief that working with people as a community is somehow inferior, there are literally no downsides, especially when you embrace the blended model. It's time to let go of being the guru and the belief that one-to-one is superior. It's not. Yes, it has a time and a place, but it also has several limitations that group sessions overcome.

In a group setting, people connect so much better. They open up. They commit more to transformation because they're sharing their experience, struggles and goals with others, even if it's only a small group. When you pack out your schedule with one-to-one sessions, you don't have a lot of free time. You can't work on your business as much as you want. You can't create as much amazing content for your clients. You can't help as many people as you want. And if you're growing a business while working another job, you may only have a few hours a week to spend on your own enterprise. Why not make the most of that time? Think about it. What's going to create the most impact and bring in the most money? Three one-to-one sessions you managed to squeeze into the week? Or a one-hour group session with 20 people? Remember, groups mean more free time for you, bigger transformations for your clients, and more revenue and growth for your business. That's why group models are king, and a blended model is a great choice. What is a blended model, you ask? Read on, my friend. I'll reveal all soon.

CREATE VISUAL CLARITY

I created the Visual Clarity Tool when I realised I was struggling to get my message across during 45-minute calls with potential clients. I tried to give them all the information about my program, but all I really ended up giving them was information overload. If someone says to you during a sales conversation, "I need to think about it," I want you to know, right now, you've given them too much information. I knew what was happening. I could see it on their faces. I could hear it in their voices. But I couldn't stop myself. I just kept rambling on about my amazing offer, leaving no insignificant detail unspoken, justifying my prices. It's natural for us to want to share all of the tools, trainings, and transformations we can give our clients, but it's not what they want to hear. Without a clear vision of what you offer, good luck resisting the urge to talk them into an information coma. Not a great way to make a sale, right? Not only have you overloaded someone with information, but they won't remember most of it. That's 45-minutes neither of you can get back. So, what's the solution? I'm glad you asked. The Visual Clarity tool solves the problem perfectly.

Creating a visual model gives you a simple tool you can use to show people exactly what they're going to get when working with you. The simpler, the better. That goes for your visual model *and* the service itself. At one point, we culled about 20 hours of lessons from the Level Up portal. Why? Because it was too much, and we wanted to simplify our strategy so people could get results quicker and easier. Sometimes, less is more. Think about it this way. If I said to you, you could get to $30k a month by watching 100 hours of that program or 25 hours of this course, which would you choose? Most people would choose the 25 hours, right? Don't overcomplicate. Don't clutter what you offer with unnecessary noise. Trim the fat. Fast-track your clients' transformations. We're looking for the easiest path to get the best results. It's that simple. Are you ready to create a visual model? All right, let's do it.

The Blended Business Model

Remember, we're focusing on a blended business model. The goal is to not only provide visual clarity for your clients but also to design a program that will provide the freedom, flexibility, and impact you want in your life. If you're not ready to implement all these things now, that's fine. It's something for you to work towards. We're about to create a scale-ready model so when the time comes to really start growing your business, you're ready to go, with the foundations already in place. Sounds great, right? Let's start now by designing your blended coaching model.

Worksheet

7

First Quadrant – One-to-One (Relationship Building)

Okay, so I know I've been spruiking groups at every opportunity, but I also believe there has to be a one-to-one element. It could be your high-ticket offer, a quick conversation at the start of their journey, or some form of reactive one-to-one interaction to reward them for the steps they've taken. It could be a combination. For example, we have an elite program for coaches who are making over $30k per month or want to commit with us for 12 months to get there. They get a one-on-one call with a coach each month to check in and get any additional support they need. For others in Level Up, we offer reactive coaching. If someone really gets stuck and group coaching calls aren't moving them forward, they can reach out by message whenever they need it to get steered back to the path of success. Also, if any of our clients hit a big milestone in their business, we book a call to celebrate with them and plan for what's next.

I'm a really direct communicator, and I don't mind baring it all in a group coaching session. But I know that not everyone is comfortable doing that. So, giving people the option to chat one-to-one when they're stuck is important. It doesn't have to be a one-hour video call. It could be a 15-minute phone call or a quick chat conversation. Whatever works for you, your business, and your clients.

Don't lose sight of people's unique needs. The one-to-one element often gets lost when big, successful companies start to scale their businesses. It's all recordings and group sessions with hundreds of clients at once. People don't feel like they're being heard and treated as individuals. Keep this in mind when designing your model.

Blended is best. Don't forget that your clients aren't just a name or a number. Sometimes, they need that one-on-one attention. Don't we all from time to time?

So, I want you to label the first quadrant 'one-to-one' and write how you will provide this to your clients. Is it reactive conversations? Is it a high-ticket offer? Is it a quick phone call once a month? Can you hire a team to create the one-on-one connection? Like I said, it should be whatever works for you, your business and your clients. But it should never overshadow your community and group sessions. We're trying to create freedom and scalability here, remember? Good. I'm glad we're on the same page.

Second Quadrant – One-to-Many (Group Connection)

Don't worry, I'm not going to spend any more time banging on about how amazing groups can be. I think my position on the subject is fairly clear. If you're still a group session sceptic – like I once was – the best thing you can do is try it. Once you start your own group program, I won't need to say another thing on the matter because the results will speak for themselves. Of that, I'm completely confident.

I want you to label the second quadrant 'one-to-many' and write how you'll deliver your group program. Is it one session per month? Per week? Or per day? If you're not ready to start group sessions yet, don't stress. We're setting you up to scale, remember? It's all about thinking towards the future.

Third Quadrant – Online Portal (24/7 Access)

Don't be put off by the idea of creating a portal or online component to what you offer. It doesn't have to be anything fancy. It could be something as simple as a shareable folder in the cloud, with videos and worksheets. In fact, that's exactly how Level Up started. We didn't have the slick platform we have today, so our clients accessed everything from a shared folder. Pretty simple, right?

Having a portal of some type is important because it gives people 24/7 access to content. It also means that clients can learn the basics before jumping into group sessions to ask questions, gain clarity, and keep moving forward. We have clients in the UK who watch recordings while we sleep. They jump onto coaching calls maybe once every other week because not all the call times work for them, but they still get access to the content and community. It's convenient for our clients and us. Why waste time repeating yourself over and over again? Record it once, and you're good to go. I don't know about you, but I hate sounding like a broken record. When I was studying to be a coach, I had to recite the exact same script, word for word, for 12 coaching sessions, with every single client. It was an amazing script and helped me learn exactly what I needed to, but it bored me to tears.

That's another beautiful thing about group sessions. Okay, you got me. I haven't quite finished banging on about the benefits of groups yet. I can't help myself, all right? Running a group program instead of individual sessions means you don't have to repeat yourself as often. Everyone on the call gets the same information at once. It's the definition of work smarter, not harder, yeah? It also lets you hold on to a little bit more of your sanity.

I want you to label the third quadrant '24/7' and write how you're going to deliver content to your clients. Remember, it doesn't need to be anything fancy. Keep it simple. Provide access to something that can be absorbed at any given moment. And, as always, aim for progress, not perfection. You can always build something better later down the track. It's what we did, and it worked out great for us.

Fourth Quadrant – Community (Building Your Tribe)

The final piece is your community. What do I mean by that? Your community is an online space that your clients can access at all times to ask questions, get support, share feedback, and celebrate wins. It could be an exclusive social media group like the Level Up Inner Circle, or it could be something different, as long as it's *something*. I love jumping into the Inner Circle every day to see people sharing big sales wins, posting workshop and program ideas, discussing pricing, celebrating success with their events, and just coming together as a real, supportive tribe. Our community is our greatest asset, and it gives our clients so much value. Don't you want that for your clients, too?

Early on, I figured that if I'm going to tell coaches they need a coach, I should have a coach too. And I do. I'm part of a mastermind, and it ain't cheap – that's for sure. But here's the kicker: I almost never see the head coach. So, what am I paying the big dollars for? *Community.* As soon as I found a community, my business went from plodding along to totally tearing it up. Why? Because we are who we surround ourselves with. I truly believe that.

Some coaches in the community are doing million-dollar months. Being a part of an amazing tribe changes the way I operate. It shifts my mindset. It pulls me out of a rut when I feel stuck. Community is so invaluable.

I want you to label the fourth quadrant 'community' and write how you plan to create a thriving, supportive tribe that will give your clients awesome value. Remember, start curating the room now so you have the right people on board from the beginning.

Once you've completed your blended business model, keep it. Refer to it. Edit it. Allow it to evolve when necessary. Don't feel like you're locked into anything you've written on paper or typed onto a page. Few things in life are static. That includes any models or action plans we create. The most important step to take with your new model is to *implement it*. Because we're more than just talk, aren't we? We're all about taking action.

Visual Clarity Tool – Step One

All right, it's time to take a look at one of the most powerful foundational tools I used to create the Level Up Formula. It's a two-step process, so be prepared to do a little legwork. Or wristwork if you're writing. Fingerwork if you're typing. Either way, let's get started.

First, I want you to answer the question: what transformation do you want to give your clients? For example, we at Level Up want to help our clients grow successful coaching businesses to create more impact, profit, and freedom by hitting a minimum of $30k per month cash in the bank. Sounds great, right? We're talking about the final transformation here, not the mini goals that lead to it. We'll discuss those next.

Now, I want you to break the transformation down into three goals your clients need to hit to get that result. For example, the first goal for our clients is to BUILD a business model so they can create a life they love while delivering an awesome coaching program. Who wouldn't want that? Next, we want them to EXCITE their audience. Once they've got their program in place, they can really start to make an impact in the world and build a community of potential – and excited! – clients around them. Finally, we want to IGNITE their sales. We help people understand that selling is just coaching. Most coaches know how to coach, right? If you can coach, you can sell. For those of you who don't coach, it's all about asking great questions so people come up with the solutions on their own. It's as simple as that.

Once you've written down the three goals that will lead to your clients' big transformation, I want you to break each goal down again into three simple steps. For example, the steps for our BUILD goal are: DESIGN a program that fits around your lifestyle. DELIVER it in a way that creates freedom for you and the biggest impact for your clients. SYSTEMISE to save time and make it easy for people to jump on board and get results. That's the first pillar of the Level Up Formula completed.

Now it's your turn. Go ahead and write down three steps for each goal. At the risk of sounding like a broken record – progress, not perfection. Don't overthink it. Write down what works for you in this moment. You can always change it later, yeah? Let's focus on taking action.

Worksheet

WORKSHEET - THE VISUAL CLARITY TOOL (STEP 1)

Goal #1	Goal #2	Goal #3
Step #1	Step #4	Step #7
Step #2	Step #5	Step #8
Step #3	Step #6	Step #9

Visual Clarity Tool – Step Two

Ah, we seem to have arrived at the final step of creating a visual model. Now's the fun part. We get to put it all together and create a visual representation that will help your clients understand exactly what your program looks like. This final step is all about slotting everything into place to create a clear illustration. Here's the Level Up visual model to show you what I mean:

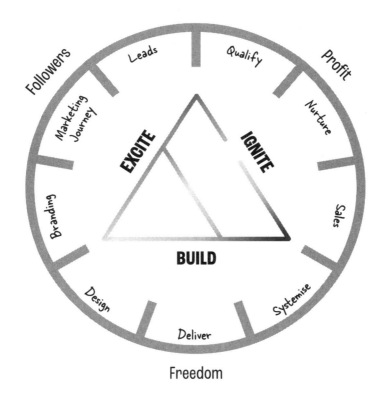

You can use the template provided or create your own. Whatever you decide to do, clarity is the goal, and simplicity is key. Got it? Great! Let's get to work.

Worksheet

A visual model will help you have clarity and confidence when talking to a prospective client and when building your hero product.

Using the goals and steps from step one, let's create your visual model now!

Once created, your visual model becomes a powerful tool for getting your message across. Don't waste time – and lose sales! – rambling on about every tool in the shed. Your visual model should highlight the important parts and give potential clients instant clarity. Put it on your website. Post it to social media. Put it wherever you think it needs to be. Not only does a clear visual model help others understand your product, but it helps with your understanding, too. Sometimes we overthink. We overcomplicate. We lose sight of what's important. A visual model helps make everything clear.

LET'S REVIEW HOW FAR WE'VE COME

Once you have a working visual model, it's time to review. All too often, I find that business owners pour more value into what they offer when, really, it's the simple and easy to use products that get the best results for clients and customers. With that in mind, looking at your newly created model, I want you to reflect on the following questions. These questions will give you everything you need to kickstart your marketing message research and sell what you do easier. Let's get to it.

The first two key questions are:

1. What is the problem you solve?

2. What is the transformation your ideal clients want?

Go ahead, write those down and answer them now. Now let's analyse the steps outlined in your visual model, the key steps your clients will take to reach their goals. Don't feel restricted by the number of steps you've listed. This could grow and evolve. Your process may require more, or it may require less. Do whatever works for you and your business. Once you've answered the first two key questions and are clear on the steps in your process, it's time to do a deeper dive into each one.

Why – Why is this part of the journey?

What specific function does each step serve? For example, when it comes to coaching, the first step often involves giving the client clarity. Consider each step and ask yourself *why?*

What – What outcomes are achieved?

What are the expected results of each step? For example, if I ask someone to create a vision board, what are we trying to achieve? Perhaps we want to gain a clear understanding of where they want to go. Consider the outcomes of each step in your program.

Emotional Benefit – What is the emotional benefit for the client?

How do you want your clients to feel at the end of each step? What has shifted for them emotionally? For example, perhaps they feel more confident after a particular step in your program. Consider the emotional benefit of each step.

Fast-Track Tool – What is your personal key strategy or tool that will get them results faster?

Finally, let's consider your fast-track tool for each step. What do I mean by this? Your fast-track tool is something cool and sexy that nobody else has. It's unique to you and your program. I'm not saying you need to recreate the wheel here, which is sort of what I did with the Unstoppable Wheels, you just need to put your own spin on the tools you use.

It's marketing 101. Make your tools yours. Make them feel fresh. Make them totally irresistible to potential clients. Let's talk Tony Robbins again. He created a multi-million-dollar coaching business and became a household name. Amazing, right? But do you want to know a dirty little secret? All of his techniques are NLP. Nothing new. Nothing groundbreaking. Just good, old-fashioned NLP. He simply took tools that already existed, renamed them, gave them a fresh coat of paint, and made them his own. And do you know what? You can do the same.

Don't stress if you're struggling to answer all the questions about each step of your process. The first time I did this, I stood in front of a blank piece of paper for two hours. *What should I do first? Is it good enough? Is this right?* Once I let go of the questioning and self-doubt, the answers dropped onto the paper effortlessly. Sure, I look back at it now and think, *What the hell was I thinking when I wrote that?* But it gave me a starting point. It gave me progress. It pushed me one step closer to my goal. Do you feel that? That's momentum. Let's keep it going!

PART 4
EXCITE

Now that we've laid some solid foundations in the Build phase, it's time to Excite your audience. What do I mean by that? We're talking marketing strategy, content, social media (if you want to market yourself online), having epic conversations, and, of course, your *branding*. How do you create a brand that people resonate with? How do you show up authentically? How are you unapologetically yourself in every touchpoint with a prospective client, in every conversation?

You need to differentiate yourself. There are a lot of competitors out there, but there is only one you. What makes you different from everyone else? What's unique about you and your journey? Most importantly, why do you want to help others? I think this is the key to a solid marketing strategy that a lot of people miss. If your audience understands your why, they understand what you are most passionate about and how that connects to them as your future clients. Remember, we're not just trying to catch your audience's attention. Attention spans, after all, ain't what they used to be. We want to Excite them into action. Are you with me? Let's make some magic happen!

Chapter 8
LEAD MAGNETS ATTRACT

Lead magnets are made up of inferior content

Debunked!

WHAT MAKES A GOOD LEAD MAGNET?

First things first, for those now asking, "What the *#$@ is a lead magnet?" - a lead magnet is a tool or resource you give away or sell cheaply so you can collect people's contact details. More importantly, this resource should show them that you have the solution to their problem. While you don't want to solve it for them until they become paying clients, you do want to give them clarity to understand that you have what they need.

Few things will excite your audience more than an awesome lead magnet, whether you're an established business or just getting started. So, what does your lead magnet look like right now? Is it in need of a little fine-tuning? Is it totally non-existent? Or do you have 20 of them that aren't delivering you new clients? Either way, we're going to dive in and discuss the finer details of a lead magnet, what it should look like, and what it should aim to achieve. Let's get cracking!

We'll start with a simple question: what is the goal of a lead magnet? You want people to understand your value when they first connect with you, right? Your lead magnet should be something exciting, something they instantly want to consume. They can't do without it! It's totally irresistible! They've got to have it now! That's why the title and wording you use is really important. It has to grab people's attention and compel them to dive right in.

With a lead magnet, you should also focus on what your ideal client wants, not on what they *don't* want or what you think they need. This, again, comes down to the wording you use. Avoid the negative and avoid any complicated words that only you, as the expert, would understand. What do I mean by that? Let me give you an example. Instead of saying *Five Tips to Get Rid of Anxiety with the Power of Multi-Dimensional Meta Programming Techniques* (which might sound cool, but I totally fabricated it), you could say *Five Tips to Create More Confidence.* Do you see the difference? You've got to hone in on what they're moving towards, not on what they're running away from, and speak their language.

It's also important to consider what your ideal client *doesn't* want to do to get the result they want. For example, *Five Tips to Create More Calm without Seeing a Therapist.* Or *Five Tips to Have a Better Day without Medication.* Or *How to Lose Weight without Giving up the Pizza.* That last one totally appeals to me. If that's your lead magnet, send it my way. What would your ideal client like to avoid doing? Would they rather not see a therapist? Do they want to avoid taking drugs? Are they really into pizza (who isn't)? Put it all together, and you've got yourself a killer lead magnet title.

Remember, not all clients will jump on board with you right away. You'll have now and later clients. So, when you give someone a lead magnet, you should also invite them into your world, whether it's an online community, social media channel, or free monthly meetup. You've got to have a community where people can hang out. You're going to have people who download your lead magnet and don't look at it for a few weeks, or even months. You've got to keep them engaged. You don't want them to forget about you, right? We regularly invite people to join the Level Up Coach Collective, a free group we run where there are free tools and trainings for people looking to grow and scale a successful business. It's all about giving awesome value, whether you're a paying client or not.

You can check out the Level Up Coach Collective by going to **levelupformu.la/collective**.

Some will eventually choose to work with us. Some won't. We never get disheartened, and neither should you. Never burn bridges. Don't think that if someone's not ready now, they'll never be ready. It's not how it works. The majority of your audience is going to want to hang out with you for a couple of months before they jump in.

Lead magnets aren't just for the start of your marketing funnel. You can add a lead magnet to your email campaigns or other steps in your strategy to entice your audience further and funnel them to wherever you'd like them to go. That's right. Even if you're established and killing it in sales, you still want to give value to your audience at every opportunity. Who knows? Attaching a good lead magnet to an email you send after someone books an initial call with you could make all the difference when it comes to closing your next dream clients. Why not push the odds in your favour?

When it comes to designing a lead magnet, it's important to let people think they can complete it on their own. Not just that, but they *should* be able to complete it on their own. You haven't built enough rapport and trust yet. They don't know you. So, if they're not quite ready to work with you, you want to make sure the lead magnet feels – and genuinely is – something they can do on their own. You want them to complete it and experience the value you can give. You don't want it to feel like a set-up, a trap. You don't want them to feel like they can't complete the task or activity without talking to you. All that's going to do is leave a bad taste in their mouth, yeah? Give them value wholeheartedly. Share some of your good stuff. Let them get a quick win for themselves. Then help them figure out the next step. Which is? To contact you, of course.

THE LEAD MAGNET BUILDER

Less talk, more action! It's time to build – or refine – your very own lead magnet. By completing the worksheet, you'll have designed a killer lead magnet that you can start using today to attract your ideal client.

Remember, you want to give them a quick win, something tangible they can visualise. You also want to use the lead magnet to address any objections they might have to working with you. For example, if time is an issue for your audience, you could mention that your program only requires a commitment of 30 minutes per day. It's important to head those objections off early.

Your lead magnet could be anything that gives value to your audience. It could be a worksheet, an ebook, or a free training. At Level Up, there's a selection of worksheets we give out to potential clients or anyone who shows an interest in what we do. Here's the kicker – they're a sample of exactly the same worksheets we use in the Level Up Formula, some of which appear in this book. We're not giving people some watered-down version of the real deal. We're giving them genuine value, and the team and I don't need to double our efforts, making different worksheets for clients and marketing. Hey, we can't give it all away for free, but we can give people tangible wins that help them understand what's possible, while leveraging our time. That's the goal.

So, it's time to fill in the blanks on the worksheet, complete the checklist, and unleash your lead magnet upon the world. What are you waiting for?

Worksheet

Who is it for?

_____
_____

What problem does it solve?

_____
_____
_____

What's the quick win?

_____
_____
_____

What do they not want to do?

_____
_____
_____

What objections might they have?

_____
_____
_____

What's the title?
Examples:
- 5 Steps to...
- Double your...
- Get more... without...
- How to...
- The 2023 guide to...
- What every person needs to...

_____

_____

_____

What's the format and how can I deliver it?

_____

_____

_____

Final checklist
- ❏ Is it high value?
- ❏ One clear win
- ❏ Instantly actionable
- ❏ Builds trust

- ❏ Fast to create
- ❏ Easy to understand
- ❏ Specific to niche
- ❏ Speaks to offer

Notes

_____

_____

_____

_____

_____

_____

Chapter 9

GETTING YOUR MESSAGE ACROSS

You should jump into paid advertising as soon as possible

MASTERING THE ART OF CONVERSATION

Conversation is an art form anyone can master. Or maybe it's a science. Really, it's a little of both. If you're chasing leads on social media or elsewhere, mastering the art/science of conversation is paramount to successfully getting people on a call to talk about working with you or buying your product online. You don't want to scare people off by getting all up in their face, but you also don't want to be too indirect and waste their time. You've got to find the right balance. What does that balance look like? I'm glad you asked.

If you're expecting a word-for-word chat script, you won't find it here. It's not how I operate. You need to figure out what works for you. Sure, I could give you a tried and true template to use, but doing so would lead to conversation mimicry, not mastery. Your conversations should sound organic, with a good sprinkling of your own flavour to spice things up. Someone else's words – no matter how much success they've had saying them – won't necessarily reflect you and your brand. However, I will provide some solid tips for mastering conversation and keeping the lead tap flowing. How does that sound? Good? Great!

First, I want to stress the fact that you need to keep it simple. You don't want to be having long conversations with people, whether it's online or in person. Why? One, because it's not a great use of your time. And two, you risk sliding into the friend zone if the interaction becomes too conversational. You don't want people thinking they can get your advice for free. We're trying to run a business here, remember? If you have long, back and forth conversations with potential clients, you might accidentally – or even intentionally – solve their problem before they've signed up to work with you. Yes, we do want to solve people's problems, but, preferably, we'd do it *after* they become paying clients. I'll say it again: we're running a business. Charity is nice, but giving too much and not receiving enough in return is a great way to run a business into the ground – or avoid getting it off the ground in the first place. Remember, we need to fill our cup to show up as our best for others. When my team and I trimmed the fat from our chat scripts and streamlined our conversations, we increased the number of calls we booked and the number of new clients we closed. I'm talking an extra ten or so five-figure clients a month. So, get to the point. Build rapport. Don't waste their time. Keep it short and sweet, and people will be more likely to jump.

9

Now for the biggest thing that trips people up: consistency. Do you have a house plant or a vegetable garden? If so, how often do you water it? Do you simply water it once and expect it to keep growing for the rest of its life? I'll tell you now – if you stop watering most plants, 'the rest of its life' won't be very long at all. The same principle applies when having conversations and trying to get new clients. You've got to stay consistent. No ifs, ands, or buts. If you want a consistent stream of clients signing up for your awesomeness, you've got to be out there having consistent conversations. Whether that's you or a team member is the next question. But let's keep it simple: consistency = clients.

Now, I'm not saying you need to spend every waking moment chasing leads. Choose the numbers that work for you. You may want to spend an hour a day. You may only want to spend a few hours per week. Whatever works for you and your business. But remember, sales is a numbers game. The more people you reach out to, the more clients you'll convert. When you reach a stage where you're leveraging your time and have a consistent revenue stream, it's time to outsource. Pay someone else to reach out to leads and book calls. This was the first thing I outsourced when growing my business, and I've never looked back.

If you use a script, be flexible. This is really important. Don't use the pre-written responses if the conversation is going in a different direction. The conversation won't flow; you won't feel good, and neither will the person you're talking to. Opportunity gone.

Make sure you're listening to what the other person is saying. Keep the conversation flowing. Don't be afraid to go off script. You might even discover a better way of saying something. If a new line gets more traction, don't forget it. Write it down, copy and paste it, play around with it. Like everything, your chat scripts can – and should – evolve when necessary. Don't get stuck saying tired old words that aren't getting the message across. The goal is to get clients on a call. If that's not happening, you need to rethink your approach.

You also need to make sure you reciprocate in the relationship. What do I mean by that? Don't bombard people with questions. Make the interaction conversational. Yes, you need to show them you're experienced in your field. However, you also want to build rapport and trust with them. It's an information swap. For example, if you ask them how their day is going, you've got to share something about your day too. Don't make it feel like an interrogation. It's a great way to have someone turn around and walk the other way.

Finally, you need to make sure you're leading the conversation. You can't expect people to magically say something you can use to get them on a call. Ask the right questions. Listen to the answers. As soon as they start talking about a challenge or pain point you can relate to your service, that's your in. Go deeper with a few exploratory questions and then offer a call. I like to say something like, "Hey, I feel this conversation deserves some more attention. I need to head off, but can we book in a time to chat further?" The whole conversation should feel natural, organic. You don't want to ask questions that are too probing, but you do want to lead them to the answers you want to hear. Remember, it's an art *and* a science. Approach conversation with a little creativity and flair, but don't neglect to experiment, test, and let the results guide you.

9

Before we dive into the fun part – creating your very own chat map – let's quickly recap the main elements of conversation mastery:

- Keep it simple

- Be consistent

- Be flexible

- Reciprocate in the relationship

- Lead the conversation

Got it? Great! Before we can put it all into practice, we should loosely map the flow of a typical conversation with a potential client. Like I said, the conversation should feel natural – you want to build rapport and trust – but knowing the terrain beforehand helps keep the discussion on track.

YOUR CONVERSATION MAP

Before we begin creating your conversation map, I want to make one thing clear. We're not creating a singular flow. You'll have different openers for different conversations, depending on how someone has engaged with you. And a conversation map is just that: a map. Just because you've got a route in mind, it doesn't mean you can't adapt to conditions and take a detour or two if it feels more natural. The destination, however, is always the same: either a call or a sale.

Your conversation map will consist of four main elements:

1. **Opener** – How you open the conversation

2. **Qualify** – Qualification process

3. **Offer** – Jump on a call, receive a free training or lead magnet, and so on

4. **Book** – Get them to book a call or buy from you

As we discuss each element, I want you to begin writing a loose script or conversation outline you can play with. It doesn't have to be perfect – we're not about perfection now, are we? – but it should help give you an understanding of how to structure your conversations. Like anything, your script should evolve over time. You may even get so comfortable that you abandon it completely and freestyle all of your conversations, which is great if it works. The purpose of this activity is to help you streamline your interactions and ensure you're including all of the essentials.

Opener

So, a potential client has engaged with or contacted you. What now? It's time to start the conversation. Keep it nice and simple. You should have several openers locked and loaded for all the common ways people connect with you. Something like, "Hey [name], what's on the agenda for today?" Short, casual, open-ended questions.

Qualify

The qualification sequence can be two or three simple questions that help provide a feeling that you understand where they're at and that you can help them. Their answers should also let you know whether they are the right fit for your business.

As an example, we always ask our audience, "So, how many clients do you want to be working with, let's say, in 12 months' time?"

"[Answer]."

"Wow, awesome. How many do you have at the moment?"

Offer

Once they pass the qualification process, it's time to put forward your offer. This could be a strategy call or a direct sale. Just remember to always sell the next step. If you're selling a low-ticket item, you don't necessarily need to get someone on a call to make it happen. Generally, however, the aim *is* to get potential clients on a strategy call and help them understand your value. Don't talk about packages or products if a call is your next step. Instead, sell what they're going to get on the call. Here's an example: "The call will help me better understand where you're at and let me make sure you leave knowing the next three things you need to do to get to where you want to be faster." One of those things being to become one of your new clients, of course.

Book

Book the call! If you don't already have a booking platform set up, I highly recommend that you get one right now. It doesn't matter if you're running a new business or you're someone with 100 clients. The secret to scaling is to plan for it well in advance. Sending someone a link to your calendar looks much more professional than pulling out your diary. It also avoids that awkward back and forth at the end of the conversation while you check, they check, and you struggle to find a time that works for everyone. A good booking platform is the one tool none of us should do without.

Putting It All Together
Remember, how you approach your conversations should reflect you and your brand. You've got to get the flavour right. Yes, you can use a map so you understand the terrain, but don't get attached to a script. You don't want to sound like a robot, right? Well, unless your target audience is keen on conversing solely with AI. But what are the odds of that?

Once you've completed your map, I want you to commit to having consistent conversations per workday. I don't expect you to be messaging people on the weekends or your days off. In fact, most people probably don't want you bugging them on weekends anyway. If you don't want to deal with chat and you are using social media or a website to chase leads, hire someone to manage your social media profiles. Do whatever you need to do to keep the leads flowing. Clients aren't going to magically appear and start asking to work with you. All right, sometimes it does happen. But it's far from the norm. If you want to convert leads to paying clients, you have to be having the right conversations. Over time, you'll learn what works; conversation will become second nature, and you'll be flooded with piping hot leads. That's what we want, right? Then conversation is something we should aim to master.

Social Media Chat Mastery

Let's talk a bit more about social media because, honestly, that's where most people are finding clients these days. I'm not saying the traditional routes aren't effective, but I wouldn't be doing my duty if I didn't touch on one of the most powerful sales tools out there.

When it comes to engagement, you should let people engage first. We're not cold approaching people. We want our interactions to be organic, not forced. So, let's run through the three primary methods of engagement on social media.

Connecting With You

If someone connects with you, you want to have an opener prepared for this specific interaction. For example, you could ask them what prompted them to connect with you. It's a great way to get the conversation started and learn more about them.

Regardless of the platform you're on, when someone connects with you, you should always screen who they are. Why? You could probably come up with a lot of reasons, but I'm talking about one specific problem. If, for example, you start accepting digital marketers into your circle, the algorithm is going to start throwing those types of people at you. Unless digital marketers are your audience, that's not what we want, yeah? Ideally, you want to show up as a suggestion to potential clients, not people who might see *you* as a potential client. So, screen before you accept, and filter out the trash.

Joining Your Group

You should also have a specific opener for when someone joins your community. You have created a group by now, right? Hey, I know social media isn't for everyone. If you've found a better way to get clients, I respect that. For those of us leveraging social media, having an open group that anyone – within reason – can join is a great way to gather leads.

When someone joins your group, you can start the conversation by welcoming them to the community. Once you've built some rapport, you'll want to ask – and answer! – a few questions and start the qualification process.

Replying to Content-Related Posts and CTA Offers

By now, I'm sure you've figured out that you also need a couple of different openers when people engage with your content-related and CTA offer posts. You'll also want to be ready to reply to any comments or questions on the posts themselves. If they're engaging with your content, they're clearly interested in what you've got to say. So, start talking!

Timeless Tips for Building Rapport and Trust

Everyone has their own approach to chatting with potential clients. Your style will almost certainly change and evolve over time as you learn what works, what doesn't, and what rings truest to your personality and brand. As we wrap up our crash course in conversation mastery, I want to offer some general tips for building rapport and trust that you can apply to almost any conversation.

Conversational tips for building rapport and trust:

1. **Ask relevant, engaging questions** – You want to keep the other person engaged, right? You also want to learn more about them and their problems so you can decide if they're a fit for you and your service. Show them you're interested – because you are! And if they throw some questions back at you, be candid with your answers. Remember, a conversation is a two-way street. You don't want to take a wrong turn and hit that dreaded no through road.

2. **Listen!** – It should go without saying, but you can't just talk at someone and expect to word-pummel them into working with you. Listen to what they're saying. Respond accordingly. A lot of the time, people just want to feel heard.

3. **Consider personality types** – If you're familiar with DISC or another personality profile assessment, you should use that knowledge when interacting with potential clients. For example, certain personality types will prefer you to be more direct and to the point, while others will want to hear every relevant detail about your offer. If you can gauge someone's personality early in the

conversation and adjust accordingly, you'll have a much easier time building that all-important trust and rapport.

SALES MINDSET

It's time to talk about your sales mindset. Now that you have your conversation map completed... You are doing the activities, right? Hm? Either way, I want to use this discussion to help you make the most of what you've already mapped or, if you're yet to nut it out, get you to start thinking about messaging and marketing.

When it comes to marketing, the Level Up Formula uses a three-step process. Your business may have already moved beyond one or more of these steps. If so, that's awesome! You can focus on the step that's relevant to you. Let's get to it.

Step One – Organic Marketing

The first step is to grow your business using one-hundred-percent organic marketing. In brief, 'organic marketing' means using a strategy that requires spending little if no money. Generally, you're at this stage when you're first starting out or haven't begun to really scale. Perhaps you're running a one-person show, and you don't have a lot of money to invest in marketing. You do, however, have a really cool idea that you're keen to make happen. You want to grow your business. Don't we all? You also want to create more freedom for yourself. It's why most of us go out on our own, right? We want to stop working for the man! We want to *be* the man, or woman.

So, the general organic cycle goes something like this: find leads, gain interest, get income. Simple, right? It's certainly a great way to start. However, purely organic marketing will only get you so far.

Step Two – Live Events
The second step is looking at marketing more widely by maximising live events. You're generally at this stage when you've hit a wall with organic marketing and need to be having conversations en masse to grow. You don't have time for organic outreach. You've shifted to working *on* the business rather than *in* it when it comes to lead generation. You're creating new systems and products – really big-picture stuff, yeah? So, how can you do organic marketing en masse to create more income, free up more time, and grow your business further? The answer is: events.

You may be asking, "What sort of events?" Well, let's list some. There are obviously in-person events like workshops, retreats, and public speaking gigs. But you can also look at online events like masterclasses, challenges, and partnering with someone who shares your audience by running sessions at their events, jumping on their podcast, and so on. You can offer free sessions, Q&As, worksheets, whatever makes sense to help people reach their goals. It's a great way to generate leads, talk to a lot of people at once, and build rapport and trust en masse. We've guided many of our members through creating their own events, and we've done plenty of our own over the years.

And guess what? They're super effective. Well-designed events will help you generate more clients with less work. That's ultimately what we want, right? The less time you're spending on chat or discovery calls, the more time you have to scale your business.

The best part about events is once they're done, if you record them, you can make them evergreen. People can access these awesome sessions whenever they want by simply providing you their contact details on a landing page or website, and you can build rapport and trust with them while you sleep.

Step Three – Scale

The last step is where you stop focusing so much on the first two steps and really start to scale. Perhaps you have a team member or two running step one. Step two, you can automate and refresh every six months or so as required. So, how do we start to scale? We're talking landing pages, paid advertising, email campaigns – just a quick word about email marketing. Anyone who says that email campaigns are dead is either lying or incredibly misinformed. Email marketing is still a brilliant way to grow a business. How do I know? I'm doing it. My email marketing campaigns get a lot of traction. I'm talking thousands of people reading my email campaigns daily. Don't disregard the power of a well-crafted email. I assure you, email marketing is alive and kicking. Okay, where were we?

When you start to scale, you bring in more money, which allows you to begin building teams and hiring help. For example, you could hire someone to do the work you don't enjoy or no longer have time for. Perhaps you want to bring a marketing manager on board so you don't have to worry about your advertising strategy anymore. You may also want to build a sales team.

From here, it's time to look at your delivery. This is where we go from one-off sales to creating monthly recurring revenue with memberships and other offers to further grow your passive income. At this stage, you really want to seize the momentum you've already created. Don't let it go to waste!

A lot of coaches like me and other marketing managers or self-proclaimed 'gurus' will tell you to start at step three. I totally get it. They're trying to give you a shortcut, which is fantastic. However, step three costs dollars, big dollars. Even if you have the money for paid advertising, there's a downside to taking that leap too early. If you haven't tested and honed your idea in the early stages, it likely isn't going to work with paid ads. The leads are a lot colder, and they don't get a direct connection with you. When it comes to scaling a business, you have to focus on steps one and two first and build on from there. It's what works for us and our clients. It'll work for you too.

I get that organic marketing can be tedious. If you're struggling with the idea, I want you to think of it this way. You're doing the hard yards now to set yourself up to hit a higher level later. That's the plan, yeah? You're testing your idea. You're interacting directly with your audience. You're learning from them. You're out in the field, researching your ideal client with every interaction. When you're ready to scale, it's incredibly easy. Why? Because you know your audience intimately, and you know you've perfected your offer. Trust me – the initial work is well worth the later reward.

Sizzling Hot Tips for Organic Outreach

Don't ask people to get into bed with you too early. Let me explain. Consider messaging someone like dating. You're not *generally* going to ask someone to jump into bed with you right away. Maybe buy them a drink first? Hey, I know there are exceptions to the rule. Let's just play along and pretend the analogy works. All right, so before you ask someone to jump into bed, you buy them that drink and get to know them first. You'll ask them questions. You'll answer theirs. You'll probably take them on a date. It's the same when chatting with potential clients. You've got to nurture your leads before you invite them into the bedroom. I mean, you've got to nurture your leads before you present your offer. I could go ahead and mention foreplay, but I think we'll leave the analogy right there.

Selling isn't about the sale. Again, let me explain. You don't want to come across as the sly fox, the used car salesman who's only focused on the sale. It's not about the money. At least, it shouldn't be. If you're thinking about money when you're having conversations with people, you're going to come across as pushy and likely a little desperate. A great way to kill the mood, right? Instead, you should genuinely get to know your potential clients because you genuinely want to help them. Success will flow from there.

Don't get friend zoned. This is important. Give people enough to get them on a call, but don't give them so much that they consider you a friend. Some people I've worked with have fallen into this trap. I don't blame them. As a startup business owner, you want to help people, right?

Giving too much is an easy trap to fall into. However, when you give too much away, you devalue your paid service. Keep the conversations short. Don't go back and forth too much. Once you've identified a pain point or challenge, it's time to move to a strategy call.

Get people onto a call. Unless you're selling a low-ticket item over chat, the primary objective of every conversation is to get people onto a call. Avoid conversing with people over email. It's a clunky way to have a conversation, and you risk overwhelming them with too much information. Also, avoid stating your prices in chat. Why? Because the person you're chatting with doesn't understand your true value yet. You've still got a little more work to do on that front. That's why we want to get them on a call as soon as we can.

Don't get frustrated with the process. Organic outreach takes time to pay off. But play the numbers, trust the process, and the energy you put out will eventually come back. The more you practise reaching out, the better your results will be. Don't expect overnight success. Hey, I'm not saying don't embrace overnight success if it happens, but don't expect it. In almost all cases, success takes time. If you get frustrated with the process, it can seep into your interactions and prevent you from gaining traction. I'll say it again: *trust the process.* Because a little trust goes a long, long way.

Organic versus Paid Marketing Strategies

What are the benefits of paid versus organic marketing? I'm glad you asked. As mentioned, organic outreach is absolutely the best way to generate leads and create brand awareness in the early stages. It's the foundation of everything that comes next. Eventually, you'll reach a point – especially if you action the advice in this book! – where you need to Level Up your marketing strategy to continue to grow your audience. That's where paid advertising becomes not only feasible but really appealing.

Of course, every marketing strategy has its pitfalls and perks, so let's put organic outreach and paid advertising face-to-face and see how they square up.

ORGANIC MARKETING VERSUS PAID ADVERTISING COMPARISON TABLE

	Organic Marketing
Cost	Free! Sort of... Organic marketing won't break the bank, but time is money, right? In the early stages of growing a business, your time – whatever you can muster – is one of your greatest assets. Where more established coaches may reach for money for marketing, you'll need to spend time instead. Eventually, you may even pay someone to do your organic outreach for you, which is a great way to leverage your time. But in the beginning, organic marketing is a godsend for anyone on a low or even a zero-dollar budget.
Efficiency	Organic outreach takes time and effort. You're not just slamming your product down your audience's throat. Instead, you're building rapport, gaining their trust, and genuinely getting to know them and their problems. Reaching out to each potential lead isn't the most efficient way to make sales. It is, however, setting you up for a smoother road in the next stage of your marketing journey.
Reach	With organic outreach, you can spend a lot of time finding and attracting leads. Sometimes, your reach will be limited by the amount of time you're able to commit to the task. Whether you're engaging in people's content, replying to comments on your own posts, or messaging people who've shown an interest in your work, you may only connect with the people who are in your direct field of vision, so to speak. In the beginning, this is fine. It's actually preferred. You won't be ready to scale straight away. You want to get to know your audience first, and that means showing up where they like to hang out, walking their walk, and talking their talk. Eventually, however, you'll likely want to expand your reach.

Paid Advertising

Cost

As the name suggests, paid advertising costs money. That's why it's so important to nail organic marketing first. You want to know your audience intimately before you start feeding your hard-earned cash into flashy ad campaigns.

Of course, the cost will vary, depending on the advertising avenue you take. The most important thing when it comes to ad spend is to *get your money's worth*. We all want bang for buck, yeah? Make sure your advertising dollars are translating to *real* sales and *real* return on investment.

In business, spending money should always lead to making money. If it doesn't, it's time to reassess and correct course where necessary.

Efficiency

Paid advertising is a really efficient way to attract potential clients to your business.

Sure, you may need to create a few different ads for different platforms and mediums. But once your ads are out in the wild, as long as you've targeted them correctly, you can simply sit back and watch the leads flow in, one after another. I mean, *sometimes* it's that easy.

However, it is sometimes harder to close a 'cold' lead that has come through an advert than a warm lead you have already built rapport and trust with.

Reach

When you use paid advertising, especially online, ad companies and social media platforms do a lot of the targeting for you. As long as you're clear on your target audience and provide accurate info, the right ads (yours) should appear to the right people (your ideal client).

Paid advertising has the added advantage of catching the attention of people who may have been in your periphery. They're still your ideal client, but they may not have been in a position for you to spot them or catch their attention before. A paid ad shown at the right time in the right place could make all the difference.

Remember, the people who you target with paid advertising are going to be colder leads than those you've identified – and perhaps even qualified – through organic outreach. This is precisely why jumping into the paid ad game too early can leave you scratching your head and reaching for that empty space where your wallet used to be. Sure, you'll learn a valuable lesson, and you might attract a few leads. But why burn the cash if you don't have to? Organic will get you a long way. It won't, however, get you *all* the way. If organic outreach has run its course for you, it might be time to fork over those advertising dollars and step up to that next marketing level.

Chapter 10
CRAFTING COMPELLING CONTENT

Posting pictures of flashy cars and private jets showcases your success and makes people want to work with you

LEVEL UP YOUR CONTENT GAME

How would you rate your content game? Are you posting consistently to social media? Are you dominating the algorithms? Are you getting awesome engagement? If you answered no to any of those questions, it's time to Level Up your content game. Are you ready? Great! Let's get into the nitty-gritty of mastering content.

The first thing I want you to know is that engagement takes time. Consistency is key. If you take a break from posting, you'll likely see your engagement take a massive dive. That's why you need to make sure you have some sort of schedule or consistent process in place.

Most algorithms won't support you if you're only

posting every now and then. Think about it in terms of earning points. The more consistently you post and engage in other people's content, the more points you earn. The more points you earn, the more highly the algorithms regard your posts. Naturally, engagement increases. Simple enough, right?

Often, organic marketing takes a bit longer than we'd like. You've got to be in it for the long haul. Don't anticipate instant success. Don't expect to go viral. It's all about taking small steps towards a big reward.

Really, you shouldn't be spending more than an hour a day on social media. Yes, put in the work, but don't make content creation the biggest part of your day. Unless, of course, you happen to be a content creator by trade. If you want to put posts out on weekends or your days off because that's when your audience is online, schedule them. It's as simple as that. As business owners, we need to make sure we're giving ourselves a break. Take time to recoup. You don't need to be working on your business 24/7. I know that's a difficult thing to say to a highly motivated entrepreneur, but overworking yourself is a direct road to burnout town. We don't want to go there now, do we?

Content Creation Dos and Don'ts

Do you know what drives me nuts? When I see coaches who are just starting out, posting photos of themselves in front of borrowed Lamborghinis and private jets, trying to make themselves look more successful than they are. I see what they're *trying* to do, but it doesn't work. Authority has to be earned. As soon as someone gets a whiff of bullshit, you've lost them. Sure, people used to love that stuff, but times have changed. Social media isn't new and mysterious anymore. Most people realise that if the grass looks too green on the other side, it's probably fertilised with a ton of bullshit (see what I did there?). So, my advice to you is to keep it real and cut the crap.

Stories make for compelling content. If you're a newbie in your field, it's all about your story. It's about your journey. It's about why you do what you do. Share stories about how you overcame certain challenges in your life if you think they will connect with your audience. In the beginning, the key is to build rapport and trust, and sharing your story is a great way to do that.

Give some value, but not too much. It's hard to know where the line is though, right? You want to give potential clients little wins. You want them to become paying clients for the big wins. What's the best free gift you can deliver through content? Clarity. Help them answer the big questions. Where are they now? Where do they want to be? How can you help them get there? Any useful tool you can offer to give people clarity is a guaranteed winner. Whenever you give value, ask yourself, "How is this pointing someone towards working with me?" If you're giving so much value that they don't need to work with you, it's time to rethink the content you're providing.

For example, if you're doing live streams every week, sharing all your magical secrets, why would a potential client think they need to pay for your service? You're already giving them everything they need on a regular basis. I'm not saying never do lives where you share your stuff, but give people the what, not the how. Show them what they need to make things better, not how to do it. When done effectively, it's a great way to give people a snapshot of what you offer without giving away the whole process. Much like this book. Yes, I'm providing you with some great tools and teachings, but I'm not giving away the whole Level Up Formula. Even if I wanted to, producing a book of that size wouldn't be practical. This book *is* intended to be a standalone resource, not a trilogy. However, there's always another tool, another teaching, another hot tip I could provide. Then there's community, which you can't get from a book. While I'm not holding back, I'm also not giving it all away. That's the mindset you need to have with your own content. Give your audience value, but always have more to offer.

You also need to make sure you're staying relevant to your niche. Your avatar needs to be on point. The topics you discuss should be relevant to your niche. I once shared that I'd been reading *The Barefoot Investor* because I knew it would appeal to my audience. Why? Because they want to make money. If, however, I shared a post about the latest video game I was playing, would it be relevant? Sure, it would be a fun topic and would help build rapport, but I would need to find a way to connect it to my audience so it stays relevant. Otherwise, I risk alienating a portion of my audience. Not exactly the outcome we want, right?

Did I already say keep it real? Well, I'm going to say it again. Keep it real. Your content should seem natural. What do I mean by that? Let me give you an example. When I'm recording content for the Level Up membership portal, if I slip up and make a mistake, I leave it in. As a recovering perfectionist, that's tough! I know for some of you reading this, I just made your skin crawl. Some mistakes are too big to ignore and do end up on the cutting floor. But, for the most part, I keep all the little blunders and missteps in there. Why? Because it shows I'm a regular person. If I can build a successful business, you can too. The alternative is a picture-perfect, flawlessly edited, slick production that makes you seem out of reach to your audience. You're only human, after all. Make sure your audience knows this.

Two Fundamental Content Categories for Service-Based Businesses

When it comes to content, there are two main categories you need to consider:

1. Authority content

2. Rapport-building content

Each content type has a time, a place, and a purpose. You'll generally use a mix of the two throughout the week. Authority content lets you assert your position as an expert in your industry. Whereas rapport-building content is all about building rapport and trust with your audience. Let's dive a little deeper into each category.

Authority Content

Authority content shows that you're an expert or authority in your space. Content could include:

- Testimonials and case studies

- Value adding (tips, tools, and strategy overviews)

- Problem-solving (discussing a client's problem you solved)

- Giveaways (worksheets, trials, tickets to your events, and so on)

Written testimonials are fantastic, but videos take it to the next level. Video content in general is a great way to build rapport and trust. A recorded testimonial from a satisfied client is ideal for showing your audience the results of working with you.

Let's talk about giveaways for a moment. Giveaways are great for getting people on board, but I don't recommend doing them too often. Sure, they're fun, but you don't want to look like you're always giving stuff away. If you're offering a reduced price – we don't say discount – for your product, make sure there's an exchange of services. A testimonial is an easy one to go to, as long as they have a positive experience, of course.

Here's an example of what a giveaway post or email might look like:

"I'm looking for 5 startup business owners who want to add $10k to their monthly revenue in the next 3 months. Would you like to learn more?"

Those who engage with the content are then told to book a call to work out if they're the right fit. If there's a match, they will receive the package for the reduced investment of $4,500, as an example. All they need to do in return is provide a testimonial at the end if they achieve the result they want.

You have to be slick with your messaging. You don't want to degrade or devalue your product, so finding the right wording is key.

10

Rapport-Building Content

Rapport-building content is exactly what it sounds like. It's designed to build rapport and trust. As a service professional, you are your brand. People will be working with you to move forward, and they want to make sure they like you first. Makes sense, right?

Rapport-building content could include:

- Debatable questions (quick posts where people can talk about themselves or give their opinions are great for engagement)

- Milestone posts about your own accomplishments (bonus points if they relate to your clients' future goals as well)

- Stories relating to your own journey (really important)

- Stories about your clients' journeys with you and what they overcame

Anything that helps clients connect with you is perfect for a rapport-building post. Once you really start to master content, you may even want to try authority-rapport hybrid posts. Don't be afraid to get creative. As long as what you're posting resonates with your audience and you're seeing engagement gradually increase, you're likely on the right track.

> ### Action
>
> Map out your weekly content themes. For example, Tuesdays could be a video. Wednesdays could be a question. Thursdays could be a problem-solving post.
>
> I've got my content map up on my wall so I always know what type of post I'm creating on any given day of the week. It helps keep me consistent. And we know how important consistency is, right?

CONTENT MINDSET HACKS

As with anything, mindset can hold us back when it comes to crafting content. You must be mindful of the strategy you choose. You need to figure out what works for you. Don't buy into what all the gurus, marketers, and everybody else says is the right or wrong approach. Most of them are likely just trying to get you to buy their products.

Go Organic

As you know, I'm a big advocate of getting it right organically before jumping into paid advertising. But not everyone sees it that way. Some people will even try to steer you in the other direction. Think about it. If a marketing agency wants you to spend money on paid advertising, they're going to bag out organic marketing so you'll buy their products, right? Whenever someone tries to steer you in a certain direction, ask yourself: What are they trying to sell me? Do they have a vested interest in steering me a certain way? Are they more concerned about making money for themselves rather than me?

Settling on a marketing plan can overwhelm business owners in the beginning. You've got so many people pointing you in so many different directions, which makes knowing the right path difficult. How *could* you know it? You may never have explored this area before. Be mindful. Consider the options. The path forward will become clear.

Let People Get to Know You

If you're marketing correctly, you should never need to pitch to a potential client. Cold calling? Forget about it. Spam emails? Don't even bother. Long essays telling people why they should listen to your podcast when they have no idea who you are? Please don't! Using these tactics will only make it harder for you in the long run. When you jump straight onto a call without building rapport and trust, you're in for a really tough time. Good luck making the sale. I'm not saying it can't be done – it certainly can – but why do things the hard way? When you content market correctly, rapport and trust build naturally, as does your audience. Some people will be ready to jump on board with you *before* you even get to a call. Yep, it happens.

I once had a strategy call with a client who said she felt like she already knew me. We'd never met before. She'd been watching my videos, reading my posts, and opening my emails, getting to know me that way. We had a fun conversation because I didn't have to explain what I did. She already felt like she knew and trusted me, so the chat was more casual. I had nothing to prove to her. If you make your content fun and really showcase your personality, the rest of the sales process becomes easy. You don't need to feel

> **The best marketing doesn't feel like marketing.**
>
> TOM FISHBURNE

like a used car salesman. I apologise to any honest used car salesmen out there. But hey, it's a stereotype for a reason.

Write from the Heart

A big component of crafting great content is writing from the heart. Trust your intuition. If you're writing a piece of content and it doesn't feel right, stop. If you're procrastinating like hell and struggling to get it done, listen to your intuition. Are you writing from the heart? Or are you writing what you think your audience wants to hear? If you're not passionate about what you're writing, it's not the right content for you. In which case, consider what else you can create. You'll know when you've got it right. You'll feel that emotional pull. You won't just enjoy creating it; you'll be *compelled* to create. Creating content should never feel like a chore. If it does, it's time to reassess, yeah? Perhaps content creation isn't your thing, and it's time to outsource. Rest assured, there's no shame in that. In fact, it may be the wisest move you could make.

Don't Write for Your High School English Teacher

When it comes to creating content, you don't need to write for your high school English teacher. Unless, of course, your audience consists entirely of high school English teachers. In which case, you should forget about progress and aim purely for perfection. This is the only time. This is a special case. This is an emergency. You don't want to catch an English teacher's attention for the wrong reasons – trust me.

I once put up a post that was riddled with spelling errors and bad grammar. And guess what? My actual high school English teacher saw it. He called me from the hospital – on a good dose of painkillers, by the way – and offered to go through the post and help me fix everything that was wrong with it. I always say, "Don't write for your high school English teacher," but that doesn't mean they aren't out there, watching, reading, and waiting for you to slip up. But hey, don't let fear hold you back. You'll never get anywhere.

Most of the time, you'll be writing for an audience that's a little less nitpicky. When communicating with your ideal client, you want to talk *to* them, not *at* them. Use their language. Talk conversationally. Avoid slang. Don't use industry terms they won't understand. For example, saying you're an NLP practitioner will have most of your clients turning around, asking, "What the hell is that?" Remember, it's all about using your audience's language. You want them to know that you understand them. You also want them to understand you, right? Clarity is key.

Do you ask your audience questions in your content? If not, I've got a big tip for you: start doing it *now*. If your ideal client were sitting across from you right now, what questions would you ask them? Put these questions in your posts, and your audience will answer them in their heads, which makes it feel like they're having a conversation with you. It's a simple way to build rapport. Go ahead, try it on your next post.

Create an Ideas Bank (or Don't)

Content just comes to me now. Good for me, right? But it wasn't always that way. When I started creating content,

I realised that I like to work in the moment. I don't use an ideas bank – but that doesn't mean one won't work for you. If I try to start a list of ideas, I find that I never look at it. It just sits there.

Instead, I'll take an idea from the last coaching session or conversation I had. This approach might work for you too. At the end of a session, ask yourself, *What did we just talk about? Is any of it super relevant to my audience? Would it make great content?* Obviously, don't talk about your clients. They probably won't enjoy that. But you can discuss any relevant topics that come up in a session. If, however, a content bank is more your style, using a notes app on your phone to jot down ideas is a great way to take the pressure off when it comes to coming up with content. Whatever works for you, yeah?

Stop Trying to Look Perfect

Perfection is a pipe dream, and trying to attain it is an epic waste of time. Progress is a much more manageable goal. The internet is filled with people trying to look perfect. Designer clothes. Flashy cars. Big houses. But it doesn't look real. Sometimes, it isn't. Not only that, but showing up on social media, looking like you've got Scrooge McDuck money makes you seem out of reach. You want to support your clients, right? You want to inspire them to reach their goals. What happens when you dangle a goal in front of them that they're nowhere near achieving? You lose rapport. People think what you're presenting is way beyond reach.

I did a public speaking training once, and the trainer said he purposely writes mistakes into his scripts. Why?

Because it helps him build rapport. If he stuffs up on stage, people laugh at him. It brings him down to their level. It builds connection. *Oh, he's only human after all*, they think. Do you get what I mean? Suddenly, he seems much more approachable. As a service professional, you want to seem super approachable, right? Well, you have to show people you're human. Because you are!

Some people spend two or three hours writing a single post – and they're wasting their time. Don't overthink it. Keep it simple. Less is more. Using simple language and making a clear point show that you're confident, professional and experienced. Your audience will resonate with your message more.

The same applies to public speaking. When we're inexperienced at doing live streams, we tend to talk more because we feel that we need to get our point across. But all we're really doing is throwing a lot of unnecessary noise in with the message. Funnily enough, it's a lot harder to do a 30 second live stream than it is to do five minutes. I've seen people just talk and talk and talk and talk and talk and talk and talk to get their point across. Do you get my point? Keep it simple. Keep it succinct. Your message will be much clearer.

Action

Commit to letting go of one belief that's holding you back with your content. Did something hit a nerve while reading this chapter? What's holding you back from reaching your content creation goals? Do you think you're not good enough? Do you think your content sucks? Do you hate creating it? Whatever the belief, let it go. Now get out there and craft some awesome content!

PART 5
IGNITE

So, you've excited your audience. Now what? It's time to Ignite them! Wait, let me rephrase that. We are absolutely *not* setting anyone on fire. Not yet, anyway. Actually, it's your sales we want to Ignite. That's right. We're going to set your sales on fire – but in a good way.

Are you someone who feels awkward about the sales process? If so, you're not alone. Selling your services – and yourself – can be one of the most daunting aspects of running a business. But here's the thing: if you do it right, your clients will actually do the selling for you. *What? How can that be?* It's hard to believe – I know. But don't worry, it'll all make sense by the end. Are you ready to discuss every red-hot piece of the sales process, from nurturing leads to closing sales and everything in between? Of course you are! It's about to get hot in here.

Chapter 11
SHARPEN YOUR SALES MINDSET

Only extroverts are good at making sales

SEVEN SALES BELIEFS THAT ARE HOLDING YOU BACK

It's time to reframe your sales mindset. What if your sales mindset doesn't need reframing? What if you have no limiting beliefs around sales? What if your sales mindset is already so sharp it's practically a weapon? Great! But having a healthy mindset around sales is something a lot of people struggle with. Even if you're happy with the way you approach selling, there's always room for improvement, right?

What's your belief around sales right now? When I say sales, what comes up for you? Maybe you're worried about being too salesy or too pushy. If so, what's the belief there? Is it that you've got to be pushy to get sales? It's a common belief. It's an understandable belief. But guess what? It's totally untrue, as are many of the sales beliefs we hold. So, what are yours?

It's time to eliminate those beliefs, the ones that are holding you back. In my years of coaching clients on sales, I've noticed a key set of limiting beliefs that show up again and again. I want to go through that list now. You may even find that some of the beliefs resonate with you. If you find yourself suddenly shouting, "Me too!" and alarming the people around you, don't worry. It happens. It's freeing to realise you're not alone, right? Like I said, a lot of people struggle with sales mindset, and many of their limiting beliefs are exactly the same.

Let's take a look at the top seven false sales beliefs I regularly encounter in the wild.

1. "I hate salespeople."

If you're someone who constantly has business coaches or marketers approaching you on social media, you may have developed a bit of an aversion to salespeople, which is totally understandable. Generally, we don't enjoy being harassed about products and services we're never going to buy. No one likes a time waster, right? I know I don't.

However, I want you to check in with how an anti-salesperson mindset is going to affect your organic marketing. Perception is projection. Remember this. If you're thinking negatively about people who are just trying to run a business – exactly like you are – how's that going to influence your mindset? You're not going to feel too great about your own sales process, yeah? I'm not saying you have to engage every salesperson in riveting conversation. Don't waste time building rapport and feigning interest. Just be polite, acknowledge what they're doing, and say you're not interested. Think, how would you like people to engage with you? You don't want them to waste your time if they're not interested, right? You also don't want them telling you to piss off. I used to get aggressive with telemarketers. Not anymore. They're just doing their job, and a little kindness and politeness go a long way.

The thing is, if you follow the advice in this book, you won't seem like a salesperson. As you may have noticed, we aim for a more natural approach in the Level Up community. We're just having conversations, yeah? We're not trying to push a product, service, or program. We're simply solving people's problems. Come in with that mindset, and you'll never feel like a salesperson again.

2. "The market is flooded."

Do you have a lot of similar businesses to yours constantly trying to connect with and harass you? It's a complaint I hear from clients all the time. "The market is flooded!" But is it? Or does it just seem that way? Let me explain.

Online, those sneaky algorithms are designed to work a certain way, right? Generally, they push you towards people you might want to connect with. That could mean people who share the same interests or work in the same industry as you. If you're a coach like me, as an example, you might find yourself being recommended to a whole lot of other coaches, and vice versa. When you've got coaches coming at you from all directions, it can *appear* that the market is flooded. Hey, you might even be right. But your ideal clients - unless, of course, they're coaches - aren't going to be bombarded with the same recommendations as you. It's all about perspective. If your ideal client is, say, a boating enthusiast, they might think social media is flooded with other people who also enjoy boats. But you may never have received a recommendation to connect with a boating enthusiast. In fact, you may not have even known that boating is something people get enthusiastic about. You're seeing the landscape (social media) from a completely different perspective. We don't all get the same view.

However, if your audience really is being bombarded with other similar businesses, so what? You're an individual. Your business is individual. While you might provide similar services to others, the experience of working with you will be different - hopefully in a good way! Instead of saying the market is flooded, I want you to think about what makes you stand out in a flooded market. What makes you an individual?

3. "I'm not a salesperson."

This is my favourite false belief. I love it. Do you know why? Because it's so totally wrong. We're all salespeople. In fact, we're selling every single day. Think about it. If you're talking to a friend trying to get a point across, you're selling an opinion, right? If you're convincing your kids that veggies are good for them, you're selling. Whenever you're trying to persuade someone, you're selling. Perhaps you're trying to persuade someone you like to go on a date. In which case, you're selling yourself. So, if you do well on the dating scene, you should be fine when it comes to talking to clients.

Hey, if dating isn't your strong point, don't stress. I'm sure you're good at selling your knowledge, your opinion, yourself in some way, shape, or form. Like it or not, you *are* a salesperson. You always have been. Sometimes, we just need someone to point it out.

4. "People won't like me."

Please eliminate this belief immediately. I've heard it all too many times before. "What if people don't like me?" You've got to stop asking yourself that question. Period. I get where it comes from. I understand what it is. When I first started out, a fear of not being liked was something I struggled with constantly.

"If I try too hard during a sales call, people won't like me because I'm too pushy."

"If I put my prices up, people won't like me because I'm too expensive."

"If I do something wrong in a coaching session, my client won't like me. They might even tell other people!"

Do you know what? It's true. Sometimes, people won't like you. It's a fact of life. You can't please everyone, right? But as long as you're being your true, authentic, vulnerable self, it doesn't matter. Why? Because you'll find plenty of people who *do* like you. They're the ones you need to focus on. The others? The haters? Are they really worth your attention? I think you know the answer.

5. "I feel too pushy and salesy."

Right here, right now, I'm going to give you the secret to eliminating this feeling altogether. The key is to look at how you're approaching your sales calls. Are you having the right conversations? What mindset do you have going in? Is your intention to be there for the potential client and serve them or are you just focused on making bank?

For example, if you believe that sales is pushy, you're going to come across as a pushy salesperson. If you're trying to push a product onto people, naturally, you're going to come across as pushy. If your main goal isn't to serve but to sell, you're going to come across as salesy. Do you get my point? It's all about mindset. You're not pushing; you're guiding. You're not selling; you're serving. You're not convincing; you're coaching. Shift your mindset, and you'll stop feeling pushy or salesy. You'll just feel like you're having a conversation.

6. "They'll just buy if I'm nice."

As a coach, I hate flattery. People who have worked with me for a while know that I don't pat people on the back and say "good job" when they haven't done a good job. You've got to earn it. I do this from a place of love. I want my clients to succeed. It's tough love but love nonetheless.

I want you to think about your ideal client coming to you for a transformation. Do they want you to keep telling them that what they're doing is really great? Or do they want you to be direct and honest with them? If they truly want to get results, they'd prefer the direct and honest approach, yeah? Now ask yourself this – do you act the same way towards prospective clients as you do towards current clients? Be honest now!

The great thing about a sales call is that people start to get an idea of what it's like to work with you. If you're all smiles and compliments and not digging into their problems, pain points and gaps, they can't truly understand what working with you is like. You're setting yourself up for headaches down the road. What do I mean? If you're all nice and fluffy in the beginning, then become really direct later, they're not going to enjoy working with you. You've basically sold them a false personality. An inaccurate picture. An inauthentic self. They're not getting what they signed up for. So, cut the flattery, yeah?

7. "I need to be extroverted."

Do you feel like you need to be extroverted to make sales? Do you feel like only extroverts can jump on camera and do live streams? Do you feel like you need to be extroverted to attract clients? None of these things are true. In fact, being introverted *or* extroverted will work in your favour either way. Why? Because like attracts like. You're going to attract people who connect with your energy. They want to work with someone who has a similar personality to them, yeah? So, be your true, authentic self. Don't feel the need to be something you're not. You don't have to fake it to make it. When you're being your authentic self, you not only attract clients, but you attract the right clients. That's what we want, right?

Before we move on, I want you to stop and check in with yourself. Do any of the sales beliefs mentioned resonate with you? Has your mindset shifted after reading this section? If not, what will you do to reframe any beliefs that are holding you back? Remember, we're not selling; we're serving. Approach every opportunity with this mindset, and I guarantee all of your conversations will go so much smoother.

DO YOU HAVE CONCRETE CERTAINTY?

Having concrete certainty is essential before you even think about jumping on a call with a potential client. What do I mean by this? Make sure you're clear on your service and the transformation you provide. Seems like common sense, yeah? Not so much. It's not uncommon for new business owners to struggle to pin down exactly what they want to offer. Hey, I'm all for jumping onto chats and *booking* calls before you have concrete certainty. But by the time that first call comes around, you better know exactly what you want to offer.

You also need to be certain about who your ideal client is. By the end of any call, you should have a clear understanding about whether you can help the person or if you need to refer them to someone else. It's okay to turn people away. In fact, never turning anyone away may be a sign that you still lack concrete certainty around who your ideal client is. Sometimes, you may only need to send someone away for a month or two to work on particular areas you've identified. That's fine too, as long as you're certain.

If you're uncertain about anything you're saying or offering, it will rub off tenfold on a prospective client.

11

They'll sense it. If you don't have faith in yourself, they won't have faith in you. It's that simple.

You don't just need to be certain about your offer and ideal client, but you also need to be certain about your on-call sales process. I kid you not – I've lost count of the number of people who have great discovery calls but when it comes time to onboard the client, it all falls apart. Why? Because the person was so focused on getting someone on a call and making a sale that they didn't consider the process for signing them up. It's as if they didn't actually expect to get a *yes*. How do you think uncertainty at sign up time makes the client feel? Like they're your first ever client? Like you're not a professional? Like they've made a terrible mistake? Yeah, all of those.

So, make sure you're completely clear on *every* part of your process, from getting someone on a call to closing the deal to the transformation you're going to give them. Consider things like, how do you gather the information to get them started? Do you book them in for their first session on the spot so they know what's coming next? Are you taking action to keep the momentum going? Are you priming them for the next steps of their journey with you?

On every discovery call, I ask two questions:

1. "How many clients can you handle right now?"

2. "How much money do you want to make in the next 90 days?"

Asking these questions does two things. One, it excites them for the opportunity that's ahead. Two, it makes them check in with the fact that they need to start working on this *now*. They're not jumping on their first coaching call unsure about what's going to happen. I'm getting them to set two tangible goals right there and then.

You also need to consider your price. Are you confident in what you're charging? If not, either lower your price or add more value until you do feel confident. Whatever you decide to charge, *you* need to believe you're worth it. To a degree, it doesn't matter what anyone else thinks. Are you confident in your price? Because that certainty – or uncertainty – will rub off on potential clients.

If you're having trouble recognising your value, I want you to write down all of the training and education you've had and tally how much it all cost. When I did this exercise, I came up with a figure of around $500,000. That's a lot of knowledge and experience I've accumulated over many years. It took time. It wasn't cheap. It has value, right? Your clients don't have the time, the means, or the desire to learn all that you know. That's why they're coming to you. Your knowledge, your experience, your transformations are extremely valuable. Your price should reflect that.

Uncrackable, concrete certainty is a key component of a sharp sales mindset. So, how solid is your certainty right now?

Action

If you're uncertain about your value and pricing, list all the training and education you've completed to get to where you are now. Figure out how much you've spent gaining all of your skills and knowledge. Also consider hours spent on learning and self-development, not just the monetary cost. How does your value stack up now?

> **When you sell right, the client sells themselves.**
>
> — JIM COCKS

Chapter 12
THE ULTIMATE LEAD JOURNEY

Sales is scary and sticky, and I'm never going to enjoy it

Debunked!

NURTURE YOUR PROSPECTS

Let's talk discovery calls, strategy calls, sales calls – whatever you want to call them calls. The name doesn't matter. What matters is the process. I'm not just talking about the process of having a conversation but also what you do between booking and taking the call. Don't forget about that in-between part. It's really important but so easy to overlook. We get so excited that we've got a call booked that we don't communicate with that person again until the appointment rolls around. By then, you've missed the perfect window to nurture your potential client.

What does nurturing achieve? So many things. It builds rapport. It keeps the momentum going. It gets clients asking to work with *you* at the end of a call. No selling needed. Sounds great, right? When done well, nurturing can be one of your most effective sales tools.

So, after a client books a call with you, what can you give them to add value and keep them focused on the journey ahead? What can you show them to help them understand you and your program better? What can you use to continue to build rapport? If they aren't super familiar with you or your content, this window is the perfect opportunity to show them a little more of who you are and what you offer. When they finally get on a call, it makes the whole conversation a lot easier.

But what can you give potential clients to achieve the outcome you want? What will bring them one step - or several steps - closer to working with you? When considering what you'll use to nurture your prospects, you should ask yourself several important questions:

- How can you provide additional authority?

- How can you further engage them?

- How can you provide social proof?

- How can you eliminate any objections?

Simple questions, right? Ah, but that doesn't mean the answers will come so easily. Let's do a deep dive into each question.

12

How Can You Provide Additional Authority?

Authority content is crucial for making you look like an expert in your field – because you are, right? Even so, if you don't express your authority, how is a potential client meant to know exactly how good you are? They can't! We know that authority building content is practically mandatory for attracting clients. But is it important in the lead-up to a discovery call? Absolutely.

Think about what you can give people to showcase your expertise. It could be a worksheet, an ebook, a free training – whatever you think will do the trick. You can even automate the process. When someone signs up to work with you, have an email automatically shoot through to deliver the goods.

It's also a great way to pre-qualify potential clients further. If someone starts working through a worksheet or training you've sent and it doesn't resonate with them, they might decide you're not the perfect fit after all. This is actually a good thing. It means you don't need to waste your time on a call that will ultimately lead nowhere. And time equals money, right? Even if you don't spend that free time chatting with someone else, you could use it to work on your business and enhance your client-getting capabilities further.

When you showcase your expertise through authority building tools, you not only increase your standing with compatible clients, but you also weed out the people who aren't a good fit. I'd call that a win for everyone.

How Can You Further Engage Them?

How can you keep people engaged *after* they book a call with you? The goal is to continue to build rapport and trust, yeah? You want them to feel like they already know you before they jump on a call. You don't want it to feel like you're meeting for the first time, even though you are. So, what can you do to keep people engaged?

I highly recommend that you invite them to join your social media group if they haven't already. Then you can tag them in a relevant post that relates to why they've booked a call with you. You're showing that you're thinking of them and that you understand their problem (as much as you can at this early stage of the relationship). They know they're at the forefront of your mind, which will put you at the forefront of theirs.

How Can You Provide Social Proof?

Anybody can bang on about how amazing their business is. But when others can't stop raving about how great you are, it holds a lot more weight. Do you have any case studies up on your website or social media you can direct them to? Do you have testimonials (video is always best!) you can send them? If you have a case study or testimonial that relates to their particular pain point, even better.

12

How Can You Eliminate Any Objections?

Objections! Not what we want to hear, right? But what if you could eliminate them before they rear their ugly heads? It would feel like a superpower. You'd approach each discovery call with a sense of total fearlessness. Absolute confidence. You'd never dread another sales call again!

So, first you'll need to consider what objections come up during and at the end of your calls. Is it a lack of confidence in the results? Is it time? Is it price? Whatever the common objections, I want you to consider how you can overcome them *before* a potential client jumps on a call. Fielding objections doesn't actually need to be a part of the discovery call process.

If people are constantly questioning whether the process will work for them, testimonials are a great way to offer social proof. You could even send them a strategy guide that covers the key components of your course so they know exactly what they're going to get. Get creative. Play around. Some objections are harder to eliminate than others, so you may need to experiment with different objection-busting tools.

Price is the one objection I would steer clear of addressing until you're on a call. The person doesn't know you well enough yet. They don't understand your true value. Until they do, your price is an empty number that could, in all likelihood, turn them away. You could, however, mention that you offer payment plans and programs at different price points. But avoid stating any prices until you're on a call, yeah? It's always best to prove your worth first.

> ## Action
>
> Answer each of the previous questions and come up with solutions. You may not have all of the answers right away, which is fine. Keep working on it until your prospects feel so nurtured they're crawling over each other to come and work with you. It would be nice, right?

MAP YOUR LEAD JOURNEY

Do you have a map of your lead journey? Do you understand every twist and turn in the terrain? Are you comfortable navigating that route with your leads? If not, it's time to map out your lead journey. I'm not just talking about the nurture sequence. I want you to map out from the point where someone first discovers you to them becoming a client. Leave no step out. What happens when you miss a step on a journey? You end up in the wrong place, lost, confused, and wondering what went wrong. We don't want that now, do we?

Don't forget to include the onboarding process: How clients access your material once they're signed on. How they arrange coaching calls. The payment process. A little tip with that – I recommend that you take payment or a deposit *right away.* Why? Because you don't want them getting cold feet and pulling out after they jump off the call. I'm not saying you don't give them an out, such as a cooling off period in their contract, but you want them to feel committed to the process. They'll be more likely to continue on to that first session and beyond.

12

BECOME A DISCOVERY CALL MASTER

So, you've got a discovery call booked; you've nurtured your prospect, and you understand your lead journey perfectly. What now? It's time to jump on a call! If you've done the groundwork, the discovery call itself should be the easy part, yeah? You're confident in what you have to offer. You've pre-qualified the prospect as much as you can. You aim to serve, not sell. What I'm saying is – you've got this.

But there's always room for improvement, right? Let's run through some last-minute tips that will make you a discovery call guru.

Be Curious

You've got to be curious. That's what a sales call is. It's about being curious. It's not selling. It's about asking really powerful questions and getting great answers. As coaches, we're masters at asking powerful questions, right? So, when it comes to discovery calls, they're just coaching calls. If you're not a coach by trade, it doesn't matter. The concept is the same. You're not selling. You're asking the right questions to get to a desired outcome. You're still coaching.

Remember, a discovery call or strategy session isn't about you. It isn't about your tools, your program, or your experience. I know that may sound counterintuitive to some people, but you don't need to justify anything to a potential client. All you need to do is understand where they're at, where they want to go, and what's stopping them. You simply need to exercise a little curiosity and try to understand their problem better than they do.

Qualify, Don't Solve Their Problems

While you're trying to understand a potential client's problems, you shouldn't try to solve them. Well, not on a discovery call, anyway. You're there to qualify, not problem-solve. The problem-solving and transformation come later. During a discovery call, you simply need to decide whether you and the other person are the right fit. If they are, they'll hopefully realise this too and ask to work with you. I repeat: *don't* solve someone's problem on a discovery call.

I know it sounds silly. But we've worked with a lot of different coaches, trainers, consultants, healers, and so on, and it happens a lot. They'll do all the hard work to get a hot lead on the phone, and they end up solving their problem right there and then – which may sound great. But now they've given away extraordinary value for free and lost 45 minutes of their time and a potential client in the process. Besides, if you can solve their biggest problem on a quick call, what could you do for them if they signed up to your program? It could be a missed opportunity on both sides.

Practise Being Silent

You may have already practised this in conversations socially. Well, now you can start doing it on your sales calls too. What am I talking about? Being silent and actively listening. More importantly, being silent at the *right* times. Let me explain.

So, you've reached that decisive moment in the call. You've shown enough curiosity to understand what the person needs. You've successfully qualified them. And you haven't gone ahead and solved their problem on the call, right? Finally, it's time to ask that pivotal question, the one that everything has been leading to: "Where would you like to go from here?"

You're expecting an answer. Any answer. It could be an, "I need time to think." But hopefully, it's a, "Where do I sign?" You're expecting an answer of some sort. What you aren't expecting is *silence*. Panic sets in. *Say something!* Your instincts tell you to start talking, to defend your program, your pricing, your*self*. But if you open your mouth, you'd be making a terrible mistake. Why? Because your soon-to-be client is processing everything and figuring out how they can work with you. *Don't* interrupt that process. They're likely solving any objections in their own mind. If you interrupt, guess who they're going to throw those objections at? That's right. *You*. Why make yourself a target when you don't have to? Do whatever you need to do, count down from ten, not out loud, that might be a bit odd. But shh...

I apologise if that came off a little blunt. But I really want it to sink in. You've got nothing to justify, nothing to prove. You've done all the legwork to get to that point. It's time to sit back, let them think, and be ready to sign them up and process their payment. Does that sound overly optimistic? Perhaps. But hey, a little confidence and concrete certainty go a long way.

THE QUICK CLOSE CONVO

Wouldn't it be nice to have a go-to script you can use to close any low-ticket sale? Well, you're in luck! I call it the Quick Close Convo. What is it, you ask? Basically, it's six magic questions you can use for a quick close on low-ticket sales. While I designed it for shorter sales *calls*, you could also use it as a chat script if it suits your style. Try it. Play around with it. See where it fits into your lead journey. Are you ready to make magic happen? Let's run through the script.

1. So, what has you interested in seeking a...

The first question will get them to open up about why they might want to work with you. You want to make sure you get some challenges out of them so you understand their problems and can move on to the next question.

2. What will it be like when those challenges are gone?

You're future pacing them here. By asking this question, you gain a clearer understanding of their needs, their wants, and what their ideal life looks like.

3. What has been holding you back from solving this sooner?

What has been stopping them? Why haven't they been able to solve their problems on their own? Once you have your answer, you should have a better understanding of what your client needs from you. Is this someone who you can help?

4. How important is it for you to overcome this challenge? Why is that?

Hopefully, they say, "Very important." If, however, they say solving their issues isn't important at all, you probably shouldn't bother going any further with them. If clearing their problems *is* important to them – why? Now you're starting to dig down to their values, their beliefs, their passions. Why do they want to make this happen?

5. How fast do you want it to happen?

We're hoping they say, "Yesterday." At the very least, we want them to be eager to get results.

6. So, what should we do from here?

This is where they ask to work with you. Simple, right?

I call it the Quick Close Convo for a reason. It really is a quick way to get to the meat of a potential client's issue and close the sale. Like I said, I'd only recommend using this script for low-ticket sales. With that said, I know coaches who have sold multi-million-dollar contracts via chat. It *can* be done. However, most clients will want a little more than a quick-close chat script or 15-minute sales call before forking over the big bucks.

The beauty of the Quick Close Convo is that even if the prospect decides not to work with you, every question they answer is valuable marketing information. By having these conversations, you gain a better understanding of the problems your audience is facing and how you can solve them. After that, it's all about adjusting your marketing to reflect what you've learnt, yeah? The more you know about your audience, the better you'll be able to speak to their needs, win them over, and solve their problems.

OBLITERATE ALL OBJECTIONS

I couldn't end a discussion about igniting your sales without addressing objections in depth. Well, I could have, but I know that a lot of people would object. Am I right?

Objections can be scary. Hell, the very *thought* of receiving an objection is enough to make many of us question what business we have running a business in the first place. But objections aren't the boogieman. They're not something to fear. We often fear what we don't understand. We fear the unexpected. The unknown. So, how do we flip this fear on its head? Ideally, we should seek to understand the objections we receive. Where are they coming from? Are they what they appear to be on the surface, or is there more than meets the eye? How can we better prepare to overcome them? Understanding *and* preparation are key. That's what this section is about: preparing for what some consider *the worst*.

Active listening. That's the first thing you need to know about overcoming objections. It's all about switching the ears on and listening to what people are saying so you can respond with the right questions.

Here's another very important point I want to make right now. One of the worst things you can do at the end of a call is ask, "Do you have any questions?" You're practically asking them, "Do you have any objections?"

So, remove that question from your vocabulary and never let it leave your mouth again. Got it? Great! Instead, we can ask, "Where would you like to go from here?" or something similar. Whatever language works for you and your personality.

12

Kick-Ass Objection-Busting Advice

All right, it's time for some kick-ass advice you can apply to any objections you encounter. We've got some serious momentum going now, so let's keep rolling.

Don't Be Desperate

Desperation stinks. You don't want to come across like it's your first sale in a month. You don't want it to seem like the future of your business depends on this one client saying yes. You don't want them to think you can't put dinner on the table if you don't sign them up right there any then – even if it's true.

So, I challenge you to meet objections with questions, not desperation. I'm not saying you should act indifferent, but a certain level of calm goes a long way.

Don't Justify

You don't need to justify anything. You're a highly successful entrepreneur. That's what you should be telling yourself. Do you think Tony Robbins or Brené Brown ever feel like they need to justify their services? No way! I want you to have that same mentality. Your perception of yourself will affect how a potential client perceives you. So, what are you? That's right. You're a highly successful entrepreneur who doesn't need to justify anything to anyone, right? I'm glad we agree.

Avoid Information Overload

Avoiding information overload should be your goal all throughout a discovery call, not just at the end when objections arise. This is why I'm a big fan of asking questions when someone objects. Instead of bombarding them with information, you're helping them solve their objections themselves. Hey, why not let them do all the work? If you ask the right questions, most objections *will* solve themselves.

Don't Assume You Know What They're Thinking

Never assume you know what a potential client is thinking. That's why countering an objection with a question is so important. You need to get down to the root of the issue, not just the uncertainty you see on the surface. Often, you'll find that the real reason isn't what you first thought. So, make sure you get all the info before offering a solution, yeah?

Top Three Objections You May Encounter in the Wild

Before we go any further, I want you to write down the top three objections you get when selling your service. Unless you're in a really unique niche, I guarantee that some of yours will overlap with the ones I commonly hear about from my own clients. Did you come up with three? Or did you come up with more? Or is there just one big objection you keep hearing over and over again? While we can't cover every possible objection here, you can get creative with the advice provided and apply it to almost any situation.

Without further ado, here are the top three objections my clients and I encounter in the wild.

12

Money

Let's talk about money. Firstly, if you have a scarcity mindset around money, your clients will have one too. I won't dive into that Pandora's box right now, but it's something I need to work on with a lot of clients. So, please work through your own hang-ups around money if you want your clients to work through theirs.

If someone says they can't afford your service, what question could you throw back at them? "What *can* you afford?" They might say they can't afford the up-front payment, but maybe they can do 500 bucks a month, for example.

By asking this question, you're lowering resistance and guiding *them* towards a solution. Don't come at them offering a payment plan right away. That's your idea, not theirs. Let them arrive at a solution that works for them.

Once someone has said how much they *can* afford, it's really hard for them to say no because they've already told you what they can pay. Just like in coaching, you're helping them solve the problem, as opposed to telling them what to do. That's the key.

However, before you address any money objections, you should ask, "If money wasn't an issue, would this be something you'd want to do?" If they say yes, then you know you've only got the money objection to deal with.

If, however, they turn around and say, "You know what? It's also time. And I don't think I can attend the coaching sessions. And this. And that," there's no point dealing with the money objection. Why? Because they're just going to keep throwing objections at you. You'd be wasting your time. Hey, they might come back later and decide they do want to work with you. But at this stage, it's best to move on because you're unlikely to turn them around.

Time

Time is another big objection people tend to raise. They either don't have enough, or the timing of the group sessions doesn't work for them.

One of the best things you can do when it comes to objections is address them before you even get on a call. For example, we run our free masterclasses at the same time as our daily calls because then we know people can attend those sessions if they become paying clients. Objection obliterated.

What's another way you can overcome the objection of time or timing? We've largely solved this one at Level Up. You can offer recordings. If someone can't make a session, give them access to the recording. Not only do they not miss out, but they can watch the video in their own time and ask questions later. It means people can absorb your coaching whenever they want. Who could object to that?

Efficacy

Will it work? It's a fair question, right? The best way to combat questions of efficacy is with social proof. I truly believe that. You could also offer a guarantee, but doing so puts a lot of unnecessary pressure on you. Sure, you *should* be able to guarantee your clients results. However, the added stress of a guarantee could affect *your* performance. And we want to be at our best, right? You can definitely make things like guarantees and bonus sessions work; you just have to be smart about how you offer them.

For me, social proof is where it's at. Not only do testimonials show that your services have worked for others,

12

but they also help potential clients future pace and see where *they* could eventually get to. When they see some guy who's just like them doing $30k per month, they realise they could do it too – and they could.

Social proof shows them what's possible. It demonstrates your value. It gives people insight into exactly what they can achieve when working with you. Once you've got them on board, the next step is to help get them those results. Because there ain't no better proof than that.

Epilogue

THE FINAL ACT

Everyone could
use a coach

Confirmed!

LEVEL UP YOUR BUSINESS, LEVEL UP YOUR LIFE

There we have it. We've mastered our **Mindset**. We've learnt how to **Build** a successful and scalable business. We know how to **Excite** our audience. We've learnt how to **Ignite** our sales. What's left to do? Take action! When you put it all together – which you certainly should do! – you've got the exact formula you need to Level Up your business and create the life you imagine.

What do you value? What do you want your life to look like? How can you design your business to move you towards that vision?

I've given you everything you need to make that vision a reality. But perhaps you want more. Maybe you're looking to Level Up even faster. Perhaps you want to be a part of a killer community of awesome, supportive entrepreneurs. The Level Up doors are always open to anyone who shares our values and is willing to do the work to get the results they want.

So, where would you like to go from here?

ABOUT THE AUTHOR

Jim Cocks is an accomplished Australian business coach with a passion for helping entrepreneurs grow and scale faster. Following a 'quarter-life crisis', he discovered his love for coaching and became an ICF accredited coach and trainer.

He has worked with thousands of entrepreneurs to help them build freedom-based businesses and offers a tailored coaching pathway to help coaches and other experts grow their businesses online.

Jim is a bestselling author and has been featured in *Australia's Best Business Coaches* magazine. His book, *Build Excite Ignite*, provides valuable insights and actionable strategies for individuals seeking to escape the nine-to-five grind and achieve more freedom and success.

clearedgecoaching.com.au

JIM'S CLIENTS

I'm Steve Wood, owner of Leaders in Mind. With Jim's support, my business thrived and grossed over $100k in three months. We teach neuroscience principles to help organisations and entrepreneurs master problem-solving and creativity.

I struggled to find the right guidance when starting out but with Jim, the Level Up team, the access to expert resources, and a network of like-minded individuals, I overcame so many obstacles. I highly recommend Jim and his team for anyone looking to succeed in their own venture.

- Steve Wood, Owner of Leaders in Mind

With Jim's support and guidance, I have now officially quit my job and got my first corporate client for training and coaching! $15k per month for at least six months. Working 1 to 2 days a week. Woo!

- Evelien Scherp, Founder of Happy Vine

I've been working with Jim for several years now. I signed up two new clients in just a week and in a year created an income of over $80k in my coaching business.

Jim has helped me in so many ways. Level Up Formula has literally helped me shape my business, from niche, to creating a course, designing my classes, the community – the list is absolutely endless!

I could talk to you for days and days about how wonderful I believe Jim is, but I want to encourage you to get on board with Jim. You will thank your lucky stars you did!

— **Sharon Kempton, Elite Performance Coach, Mentor, and Opera Diva!**

Thanks to Level Up and Jim's coaching, we generated additional sales of $9,000 in the last two weeks. He's been awesome. I love working with him and can't wait to see where the business goes next!

— **Ange Ritchie, Founder of My Goal Squad**

Thanks to Jim's 'Creating Killer Content' videos, I was able to up my price to $6k and attract my ideal client effortlessly. By getting clear on my niche and positioning myself as an expert, I was able to have easy conversations and make quick sales. Thank you, Jim, for helping me achieve this level of success!

— **Sherren Edkins, Leadership Coach**

Thanks to the Level Up Formula tools and branding expertise offered by Jim, I was able to transform my struggling hypnotherapy/coaching business into a thriving full-time practice. In just one week, I generated an incredible $11,000 in revenue! I can't thank Jim enough for his invaluable support and guidance.

— **Nichola Davenport, Mindset Coach and Hypnotherapist**

Working with Jim was a pivotal moment in my life transformation and business journey. The biggest takeaway is to not cast a wide net and get real results that matter for clients. Which is what I got from Level Up.

— **Anthony Joel, Career Coach**

I secured $10k for Grounded Women Gardening. So excited! Thanks, Jim, and the Level Up team, for all your coaching and support.

- Rebecca Dyson Tichbon, Integrative Health Coach

I just signed a new client using the ultimate sales script! Deposit paid, and she will pay in full before the first session. She read a book that recommended getting a coach to overcome common traits for women in their careers. The stars aligned!!

- Tracey Leslie, Mindset Coach

I recall meeting you (Jim) years ago, when you were speaking excitedly about a new business program. Despite my initial thoughts, I soon came to admire your passion and dedication. Working with you has been a privilege, and I have been fortunate to witness your ability to change lives. Your Level Up Formula has certainly impacted me, and I wish you all the best, my mentor and friend.

- Amber Duscher, The Retail Sales Coach

Launching my single and ready for love five-week online group coaching program, I signed up five people, which I was excited about... however... Thanks to Level Up, I've been very consistent with posting content surrounding this topic and have received three brand-new sign ups!! I'm so excited. Now I need to get myself into gear.

- Stela Ili, Relationship Coach

My life has completely transformed since I started working with Jim. I was on the brink of giving up on my business, but Jim's guidance and motivation helped me turn things around. In just six months, I have made over $10,000 – something I never thought was possible. Jim's constant hand-holding and belief in me gave me the push I needed to keep going. I'm truly grateful for his support and can confidently say that he saved my life.

Thank you, Jim, from the bottom of my heart. I look forward to continuing to work with you and achieving even greater success in the future.

— **Marcel, Founder of Enlighten My Health**

Working with Jim has been life-changing! With his coaching, I increased my income from $300 to $4000 fortnightly. His structure, community, and support gave me clarity, direction, and confidence in my business. I'm now prioritizing and impacting others. Thank you, Jim!

— **Jess Burchell, Financial Educator and Mindset Coach**

Transformed my coaching business with the 12-month package! Clients want to work with me longer, and my sales have never been better. Highly recommend this game-changing approach!

— **Howard Blackburn, Founder of Pathrive**

I never thought I could get paid for my expertise, having grown up in a small town, where volunteering was the norm. But after working through my mindset blocks and putting myself out there, I'm thrilled to say I just landed my first paying client with my new package! The Level Up Formula has been a game changer for me, and I can't thank Jim enough for his guidance and support. It's amazing to finally be seen as an expert in my field and be compensated for it. I can't wait to see where this new venture takes me!

— **Helene Steward, High Performance Coach for athletes**